EXPLORE the BIBLE

ADULT
COMMENTARY

1 Corinthians

E. LeBron Matthews

JUNE, JULY, AUGUST 1997

Volume 1, Number 4

THE SUNDAY SCHOOL BOARD

ADULT COMMENTARY

PRODUCTION TEAM
BEN GARNER
Editor

CAROL DeMUMBRUM
Graphic Designer

MELISSA FINN
Technical Specialist

JANET BELCH
Production Specialist

BUELAH V. THIGPEN
ROSS H. McLAREN
Biblical Studies Specialists

Send questions/comments to
Ben Garner, Editor
127 Ninth Ave. North
Nashville, TN 37234-0175

MANAGEMENT PERSONNEL
RICK EDWARDS
Manager, Adult Biblical Studies Section

LOUIS B. HANKS
Director, Biblical Studies Department

BILL L. TAYLOR
Director,
Bible Teaching-Reaching Division

Explore the Bible: Adult Commentary (ISSN 0164-4440) is published quarterly by The Sunday School Board of the Southern Baptist Convention, 127 Ninth Avenue, North, Nashville, Tennessee 37234: James T. Draper, Jr., President; O. Eugene Mims, Vice-President, Church Growth Group; Bill L. Taylor, Director, Bible Teaching-Reaching Division. Printed in the U.S.A. If you need help with an order, WRITE Customer Service Center, 127 Ninth Avenue, North, Nashville, TN 37234-0113, FAX (615) 251-5933; or EMAIL to 70423,2526@compuserve.com. Mail address changes to: *Explore the Bible: Adult Commentary*, Customer Service Center, 127 Ninth Avenue, North, Nashville, TN 37234-0113. © Copyright, 1996, The Sunday School Board of the Southern Baptist Convention. All rights reserved.

Explore the Bible

IN THIS ISSUE

* Evangelistic Lesson

Introducing
1 Corinthians

People often think of first-century churches as being ideal. This was not the case. Churches then were like churches today; they had problems. Some, like the church at Philippi, had relatively few problems. But others had many serious problems. Perhaps the congregation with the most difficulties was that in Corinth. It certainly was not a church that could be a model for modern congregations. First Corinthians is one of a series of letters that Paul wrote in an effort to correct the problems in the local church at Corinth.

The City of Corinth

Corinth was the capital of the Roman province of Achaia. After the Roman conquest of Greece in 196 B.C., Corinth was declared a Roman-free city. The Greeks interpreted this declaration to mean independence of action. Realistically, however, the city had the privilege of self-government; but freedom was limited to that enjoyed by a client within the relationship to the patron. The freedom of Greek cities existed only when such freedom did not conflict with the city's greater status of servitude to Rome.[1]

Estimates for the population of Corinth vary, but somewhere between a half million to one million seems reasonable. By Paul's time Corinth was a senatorial province whose population included Romans, Greeks, Syrians, Asiatics, Egyptians, and Jews. For the most part this medley of races had retained the worst features of the original stocks.[2] The language was, in the main, Greek.

The city was not situated in a fertile valley, but on the unfertile soil of an elevated plain overlooking the Isthmus of Corinth. This narrow strip of land, 10 miles long and 4 to 8 miles wide, connected the southern Greek peninsula with the Greek mainland. All north-south overland travel was funneled through Corinth.

The sea gave the city its glory. The city was located between two seaports. To the north was the Gulf of Corinth, 78 miles in length. This body of water opened into the Mediterranean Sea just south of the Italian boot. On its shore was the little port city of Laechaeum, the gateway to such destinations in the west as Italy and Spain. On the other side of the isthmus was the Saronic Gulf with the port town of Cenchreae.

Because of the dangerous journey around the tip of Greece, most cargo was hauled overland between the two ports. These port cities were the main source of income for Corinth. Some larger ships unloaded all goods in one of the ports. The goods were transported across the isthmus and loaded on board another ship. Some smaller ships were hauled across the isthmus on the *diolkos,* or "haul-across," a tram of rolling timbers.[3]

Other economic resources included limited farming. The city was a major banking center for the eastern region of the Roman Empire. Slavery was an important part of the city's revenue.

Corinth was a city of vice and paganism. Corinthians were stereotyped in the first century as immoral alcoholics. Diverse religions from various parts of the Roman Empire found a home in Corinth. Apollo, Hermes, Heracles, Athena, and Poseidon had temples located in the city.

Aesclepius, the Greek god of healing, was prominent in Corinth. A temple to him and his daughter Hygieia stood at the northern edge of the city. Pilgrims came to Corinth from great distances for treatment.[4] They left terra cotta replicas of the body parts that had been healed.[5]

Without a doubt the most famous cult in the city was that of Aphrodite. This Greek goddess was identified with the Roman goddess Venus and the licentious Phoenician deity Astarte. By the time Paul arrived in the city, her name was synonymous with sexual intercourse. Her temple was located in the most prominent location and at one time was staffed by 1,000 prostitutes! These women served as public harlots in the official prostitution before the altar of the goddess. At night these slaves plied their trade in the streets for profit.

Beginnings of the Church in Corinth

Between January, A.D. 49, and January, A.D. 50, the Roman Emperor Claudius expelled all Jews from the city of Rome. The edict expelling them stated that the reason was because of a certain Chrestus, who constantly had caused unrest.[6] Most likely, the trouble was the proclamation that the crucified Jesus of Nazareth was the Christ. The faith had reached Rome as Christian merchants traveled the routes of trade and commerce carrying their faith with them.

Aquila and Priscilla, a married couple, were among those Jews expelled from Rome (Acts 18:2). They were tentmakers by trade and worked with Paul to earn their living (Acts 18:3). Presumably, they already were Christians when they arrived in Corinth. After the mixed response Paul received in Athens, he traveled to Corinth. He arrived in February or March, A.D. 50. He quickly became friends with Aquila and Priscilla.

Paul worked as a tentmaker, preaching only on the Sabbath in the synagogues. Later, Silas and Timothy joined him; and Paul then devoted his full attention to his ministry. His preaching created a radical break with the synagogue. Paul dramatically left and established a Gentile church in a house adjacent to the synagogue. Among the converts was Crispus, the leader of the synagogue (Acts 18:8; 1 Cor. 1:14).

Trouble followed. The Jews charged Paul with breaking the law and carried him before the Roman governor Gallio. Gallio was the son of Marcus Annaeus Seneca, a Spanish orator and financier, and the elder brother of the philosopher Seneca. He served as proconsul of Achaia from May 1, A.D. 51, to May 1, A.D. 52. He disliked the climate in Corinth and so returned to Rome as an advisor to Nero.

The governor refused to hear Paul's case. He considered the charges to be strictly an internal Jewish religious affair. Because of his refusal, Sosthenes, the synagogue ruler, was beaten in front of the proconsul's eyes. But Gallio remained indifferent. His refusal set an important precedent that would be followed in other provinces. Christianity would not yet be appraised as a new religion having no lawful status within the empire. Christians could continue to enjoy the protection afforded to them by their legal status as members of a Jewish sect.

Soon thereafter, Paul departed Corinth and traveled to Ephesus. He had spent 18 months in the city. During that time, he established a church. The church continued to flourish after his departure, but serious problems began to develop.

Aquila and Priscilla also went to Ephesus. They instructed an eloquent Alexandrian named Apollos about the specifics of the gospel. When he desired to travel to Achaia, the Ephesian congregation wrote him a letter of introduction. He then became pastor of the church at Corinth (Acts 18:24–19:1).

1 Corinthians

Paul's Contacts with the Corinthians—After Paul left Corinth he maintained contact with the church there. During his third missionary journey, Paul returned to Ephesus and ministered for about three years. During that time, he had numerous contacts with the Corinthian church.

1 Corinthians actually is the second letter Paul wrote to the church in Corinth. During the interval he was in Ephesus, a series of reports on problems and divisions in the church at Corinth reached the apostle through Chloe's people (1 Cor. 1:11). Paul wrote a letter that no longer exists and addressed the problems (1 Cor. 5:9). This correspondence seems to have had little impact. Soon thereafter, the Corinthian congregation wrote Paul a letter containing questions about certain problems such as fornication and misconduct in public worship (1 Cor. 7:1). Later, a delegation from the church was sent to Paul for additional information (1 Cor. 16:17). Sometime during this period, Apollos quit his ministry in Corinth and returned to Ephesus. Paul urged him to return to Corinth, but he re-

fused to be persuaded by Paul's appeals (1 Cor. 16:12).

Paul next sent Timothy and Erastus to Macedonia and Corinth (Acts 19:22; 1 Cor. 4:17). Then he wrote 1 Corinthians (his second letter to this church). He sent the letter so that it would arrive before Timothy (1 Cor. 16:8). Timothy rejoined Paul after an apparent failure at Corinth (2 Cor. 1:1). Paul, in sorrow, made a brief but fruitless visit to Corinth (2 Cor. 2:1; 12:14; 13:1).

In the Spring of A.D. 55, Paul wrote a third letter containing a strong rebuke to the Corinthian church (2 Cor. 7:8). He sent Titus, who had become his "trouble-shooter," with this letter (2 Cor. 8:6,16-17). Paul waited on Titus to return but became impatient and left Ephesus for Corinth. In Troas there was an open door for his ministry; but because of the problems at Corinth, Paul had no heart for the work and did not preach (2 Cor. 2:12). In Macedonia Paul met Titus, who reported a reformation in the Corinthian church (2 Cor. 2:13; 7:6). Apparently, the letter had the desired effect (2 Cor. 7:9). After receiving the good news, Paul wrote 2 Corinthians.

While in Philippi, Paul collected money for the widows and orphans in Jerusalem. He bragged about the Corinthian effort already being complete (2 Cor. 9:2). Paul continued his travel and stayed that winter in Corinth. During his stay in the city, Paul wrote his epistle to the Romans.

Material—Paul's normal practice was to cover doctrine first and then ethics. In 1 Corinthians he presented ethics first, followed by doctrine. Some of the material covered in this letter was in response to questions asked by the Corinthians. The questions no longer are known, but the essential content of some can be reconstructed.

Author—The apostle Paul wrote 1 Corinthians from Ephesus. The date was probably was A.D. 53.

Contents—Basically 1 Corinthians has two parts. The first concerns the report of Chloe's people (1:1—6:20). The second concerns questions raised in the letter to Paul from the Corinthian church (7:1—16:24). The letter contains practical instructions and information for the church.

1 Michael Grant, *History of Rome* (New York: Charles Scribner's Sons, 1978), 136.

2 Leon Morris, *The First Epistle of Paul to the Corinthians: An Introduction and Commentary, Tyndale New Testament Commentaries,* ed. R. V. G. Tasker (Tyndale Press, 1958; Grand Rapids: Wm. B. Eerdmans, 1958), 15.

3 The *Interpreter's Dictionary of the Bible,* 1962 ed., "Corinth" by Jack Finegan, 1:682.

4 Otto F. A. Meinardus, *St. Paul in Greece* (Athens, Greece: Lycabettus Press, 1973), 64.

5 *Holman Bible Dictionary,* s.v. "Corinth" by Glaze, 300.

6 Suetonius, Life of Claudius, 25:4 (ca., late first century A.D.), quoted in Eduard Lohse, *The New Testament Environment,* trans. John E. Steely (Nashville: Abingdon, 1976), 204.

Focusing on What Unites Us

Background Passage 1 Corinthians 1—4
Focal Passages: 1 Corinthians 1:10-13; 3:3-6,16-17,21-23

Introduction

As members recounted better days, tears rolled down the faces of the small congregation. What had caused their grief? Long ago a habit of conflict had emerged in the church. Regardless of the issue, a familiar pattern had developed. When a controversy arose, and people took sides behind opposing church leaders. Finally, one group left and joined another church. Only a handful remained. On this day the "Amen" of the benediction rang with a finality never felt before. Outside, everyone watched as the pastor locked the door for the last time. They lingered for what seemed like an eternity. Eventually, they left one by one; and another church passed into history.

Could this happen to your church? Sadly, the answer to the question is yes. It happens too often. Divisiveness will destroy a family, or a Sunday School class, or a church. Focusing on the basic unity in Jesus Christ prevents such tragedy.

1 Corinthians 1—4
  1. Paul's Greeting (1:1-9)
  2. Divisions in the Church (1:10-17)
  3. God's Wisdom and Human Wisdom Contrasted (1:18–2:16)
  4. Viewing Church Leaders in Proper Perspective (3:1–4:21)

The Background

Paul established the church at Corinth on his second missionary journey. After a ministry there of 18 months, he departed for Syria. Paul's hosts in Corinth, Priscilla and Aquila, traveled with him as far as Ephesus. At Ephesus the couple met a dynamic but inexperienced preacher named Apollos, whom they instructed further in the Christian faith. Then the church at Ephesus sent him to minister in Corinth (Acts 18:18–19:1).

Apollos was still in Corinth when Paul returned to Ephesus on his third missionary journey. Certain problems and dissensions surfaced in the Corinthian congregation. Shortly thereafter, Apollos returned to

Ephesus. Whether the trouble or something else caused his departure is unknown. But Apollos declined Paul's suggestion that he return to Corinth (16:12). Meanwhile, Paul increasingly was drawn into the conflict in this church that he founded and nurtured through much work and time.

In an effort to resolve the strife, Paul wrote 1 Corinthians. The first issue that he addressed was the formation of factions in the church. Paul encouraged the Corinthians to focus on their unity in Christ rather than dividing up behind certain leaders (1:10-17). Rather than idolize human leaders, church members needed to dedicate themselves to Christ alone (3:16–4:21). Genuine Christian unity exists only where everyone honors Christ for the salvation they have received.

The Lesson Passage

1. Paul's Greeting (1:1-9)

Paul used the customary form for introducing letters in the first century A.D. First, he introduced himself and Sosthenes as the ones who sent the letter. Sosthenes may have been the ruler of the synagogue who persecuted Paul before the Roman governor Gallio. If so, Sosthenes became a Christian after the riot that followed the hearing. Next, Paul identified his readers as members of the church in the city of Corinth. Then he greeted them. Paul combined the Gentile greeting "grace" with the Jewish salutation "peace" and made a distinctive Christian point. Peace always follows grace.

The greeting was followed by a prayer of thanksgiving for the church at Corinth. Paul was thankful that the Corinthians had received the grace of God. He was glad they had been enriched in God. And Paul rejoiced that the Corinthians had received spiritual gifts from God. The gifts were so generous that the church members were not lacking anything they needed to do Christ's work.

Paul concluded his introduction with a note that God's character produced harmony. God called the church "into fellowship with His Son, Jesus Christ." Everyone called Him "Lord." If unity exists between Christ and an individual, solidarity continues between that person and other members of Christ's body, the church.

2. Divisions in the Church (1:10-17)

Paul had learned of divisions in the church at Corinth. Divisions in a church, wherever it is or in whatever century, cause damaging effects to a church's ministry that may endure for many years. Paul immediately sought to make his readers aware of the effect their words, attitudes, and actions had on the congregation's unity.

Verse 10: *Now I exhort you, brethren, by the name of our Lord Jesus Christ, that you all agree and that there be no divisions among you, but that you be made complete in the same mind and in the same judgment.*

God called the church to unity, but divisions existed in Corinth. The verb **exhort** literally means "to call along to the side of." The actual sense of the word is determined by the context, the status of the one doing the calling, and the nature of the calling. When used in prayer, the word was a call to God for help. Or the word could refer to calling an attorney for legal assistance. Another meaning of exhort is "to beseech." This meaning was similar to invoking divine help, but the one addressed was not one's superior. For example, in the first century the word described an army officer offering encouragement to his soldiers.

In the New Testament the word *exhort* often has the sense of exhortation based on salvation.[1] Hence, Paul called on the Corinthians to come stand at his side. He based the demand on the established fact of their salvation! Paul reinforced his appeal by addressing the readers as **brethren.** They shared with Paul a common faith and family relationship. This oneness was greater than the differences caused by the split.

Paul began his exhortation by pointing to facts everyone accepted. In biblical usage **the name** of the **Lord Jesus Christ** was more than an identification. It referred to His nature. Thus, Paul indicated that the various groups accepted certain fundamental truths concerning Christ. They agreed that these truths implied that unity should exist in the church. Although disruptive dissension typified the congregation, the church had not yet dissolved or broken apart. Therefore, Paul used medical terminology to characterize their distress. They needed to **be made complete.** This verb described setting a bone so that it might be restored to its useful condition. The church needed to unite and to become wholly one in love and in purpose.

Verse 11: *For I have been informed concerning you, my brethren, by Chloe's people, that there are quarrels among you.*

Paul had learned of the situation in Corinth from **Chloe's people.** Chloe was the nickname of the Greek goddess Demeter. The same name often was given to slaves. However, this Chloe either owned her own slaves or employed free persons. Neither the location of her home nor how her people learned of the situation in Corinth is known. Chloe apparently lived in Ephesus or Corinth. If the former is correct, then these individuals returned home after a visit to Corinth and informed Paul of the situation there. If the latter is accurate, then the information arrived in Ephesus when they visited from Corinth. Whether Chloe herself was a Christian is not clear. Individuals in her household certainly were believers. Whatever their specific circumstance might have been,

Chloe's people informed Paul that the church in Corinth was tormented by a number of disagreements.

Verse 12: *Now I mean this, that each one of you is saying, "I am of Paul," and "I of Apollos," and "I of Cephas," and "I of Christ."*

The congregation had formed four divisions within the church. Each party claimed a preference for a particular leader. Paul gave value and validity to the ministry of each leader (see 3:6). He knew these leaders were not responsible for the actions of those people who claimed to follow them. Paul called the believers to abandon their slogans and sectarian spirit.

The first group named said *"I am of Paul."* Paul did not sanction this group. The presence of Paul's name at the top of the list may show his abhorrence in having it used in such a divisive manner!

A second party was crying *"I of Apollos."* Apollos was an eloquent preacher (Acts 18:24-28) and had become pastor of the church after Paul. This letter reflects Apollos's personal popularity in Corinth and his followers' loyalty.

A third division asserted *"I of Cephas."* Cephas was Aramaic for the name Peter. Simon Peter may have visited Corinth, or the Corinthians may have known him by reputation. The group's origin is unknown and is, in fact, a moot point. It existed, and the group should not have been allowed to continue!

The fourth group stated *"I of Christ."* Possibly, these people were simply tired of the other three parties. However, their presence in the series of parties insinuates a negative identification. Some scholars have assumed that the party of Christ probably was an early form of gnosticism. Followers of this heresy said that the earthly Jesus was unimportant; the divine Christ was important. Whoever this party was, they apparently thought they were more spiritual than the other three groups.

Verse 13: *Has Christ been divided? Paul was not crucified for you, was he? Or were you baptized in the name of Paul?*

After listing the four divisions, Paul asked three rhetorical questions. A yes answer was an absolute impossibility. Therefore, no was the obvious answer to each query. Christ cannot be divided. Only Christ could redeem sinful humanity. Baptism in the name of someone identified commitment to that person.[2] Christian baptism necessitates loyalty to Christ. Paul's question may manifest an overemphasis on baptism by the Corinthians. They may have given too much credit to the one administering the ordinance, to the ritual's significance, or to both.[3]

The church is the body of Christ, not a body of Christians. Divisions in the church are as absurd as a yes answer to Paul's questions!

Paul reflected on his ministry while in Corinth. He mentioned some specific individuals whom he had baptized (1:14-16) but summarized his major purpose as preaching on the crucifixion of Jesus (1:17). Paul's denial of baptizing most of them indicated that he did not believe there was saving power in the act of baptism. Also, Paul did not believe that the agent of baptism had any special importance. Paul was particularly concerned that no one iln the church claim that he or she was baptized in his (Paul's) name.

3. God's Wisdom and Human Wisdom Contrasted (1:18–2:16)

Christian preaching seems foolish to most people. God's Son becoming a man and dying on a cross does not make sense, they say. However, the cross of Christ *is* God's wisdom even if the world's masses judge the gospel message as absurd.

Wisdom is the application of knowledge. Jewish society of Paul's day appraised the practical function of religion in daily living as wisdom. The Greeks preferred a philosophical system of thinking. Neither enabled people to know God. Salvation cannot be achieved by human effort, nor can one know God by mental exercise. God can be known because He reveals Himself to people.

The Jews demanded that Paul prove the truth of his message. To their way of thinking, the idea of Deity submitting to the curse of crucifixion was impossible. The concept of a crucified Messiah was foreign to their way of thinking. According to Deuteronomy 21:22-23, the one who died by hanging on a tree was "accursed of God." Therefore, crucified and Christ were contradictory terms!

The Greeks laughed at the gospel They believed that whenever their pagan gods took human form, the gods made life hard on people. These gods, the Greeks thought, seduced women, injured men, and destroyed property. The Gentile world could not comprehend a God who would allow such treatment of His only Son. They tried to analyze the message. They wanted it to conform to human logic. It did not.

The gospel of Christ cannot be harmonized with human intellect. The majority of those who hear the gospel reject its message because it seems foolish. But those who believe are changed permanently. The world alleges them to be foolish, but God proves them wise.

Paul offered his own example as evidence of the power of the gospel. Apparently, he was not a good speaker. His preaching was neither polished nor clever. He knew his limitations as a public speaker. Yet, the church at Corinth was evidence of the success of Paul's message. The Corinthian church rested on God's power, not Paul's oratory.

4. Viewing Church Leaders in Proper Perspective (3:1–4:21)

Jesus described conversion with the phrase "born again" (John 3:3).

His words imply that a new Christian is an infant. The food of a baby is milk; a newborn child cannot swallow solid food without choking. Older children require more nourishment and eat solid food. The Corinthians were like spiritual infants; their diet was spiritual milk only. Paul pointed out to the believers that the divisions among them gave evidence of their spiritual immaturity. Disunity most often is caused by spiritual infancy.

Verse 3: *for you are still fleshly. For since there is jealousy and strife among you, are you not fleshly, and are you not walking like mere men?*

Terms such as *fleshy* and *men* emphasize that the Corinthians were like sinful humanity. Worldly instincts still dominated them. Both *jealousy* and *strife* were deeds of the flesh (Gal. 5:19-21). Although the Corinthians were indwelt by the Holy Spirit, they were not yielding to His control. Hence, they were not maturing in the Christian life. Little if any distinction could be perceived between them and the pagans living around them. Both lived a self-centered life. They were controlled by self-interest rather than the Holy Spirit.

Verse 4: *For when one says, "I am of Paul," and another, "I am of Apollos," are you not mere men?*

Perhaps Paul named himself and Apollos because less tension existed between the two. A more plausible reason was the firsthand companionship they enjoyed. Both Paul and Apollos were in Ephesus. (Peter likely was in Jerusalem, unaware of the dissension.) Paul, however, did not blame Apollos or himself. The fault was with the people. They were taking sides in a rivalry that did not exist!

Verse 5: *What then is Apollos? And what is Paul? Servants through whom you believed, even as the Lord gave opportunity to each one.*

Paul used the word *what,* not who. He asked what was the function of Apollos, and what was the role of Paul? In the first four verses of this chapter, Paul had described the evils that resulted from preoccupation with individuals. In this verse he moved the reader's attention away from the personalities of Paul and Apollos and focused on the two minister's roles within the congregation. Christians sometimes need to remember their purpose in life rather than what status they hold.

Servants referred to table waiters and household servants. Servants were people who helped other people. The Greek word literally means "through dust." It suggests the raising of dust as a servant hastened to wait upon a master.[4] The word stressed both the lowly nature of serving and the useful service rendered. God was the Master of His house. Paul and Apollos were mere servants in the house. For a guest to give more attention to servants than to the host was an insult. The Corinthian Christians should have been giving most attention to Christ and not to His servants, Paul and Apollos.

The phrase **through whom you believed** reminded the Corinthians that they were saved because they listened to Apollos or Paul preach. The Lord **gave opportunity to each** man. The two missionaries had arrived in the city preaching Christ crucified and risen, and God had saved those who were privileged to hear the message and who believed the message about Christ.

Verse 6: *I planted, Apollos watered, but God was causing the growth.*

Paul changed the analogy from household servants to the duties of servants working on a farm. The tasks of the two were closely related to God's work. Paul's and Apollos's work could be distinguished from God's work but not separated from God's work. Neither the one who planted the seed nor the one who watered the soil caused the plant to grow. Thus, God's activity could not be separated from the respective labor of Paul and Apollos. Each of the two men did his assigned duty, but God brought the final outcome. While it took both men's labor to produce a successful garden, in reality neither was critical. Only God could produce results.

Numerous biblical and historical examples demonstrate the effectiveness of the believer's work and God's work. For instance, Moses brought Israel out of bondage in Egypt. Joshua then brought them into Canaan. The beginnings of the foreign missions movement among Baptists in America was based on two parallel efforts—Adonarim Judson labored overseas while Luther Rice raised funds in the United States. Today, church starters begin new churches. These congregations grow under the leadership of a bivocational mission pastor. Eventually, the church membership grows large enough to support a full-time minister. The ultimate success, however, is due to God, not the various ministers who have served.

Although Christians cannot effect growth, they are responsible for doing the tasks God assigns to them. They will be judged accordingly. Some will receive rewards. Others will enter heaven but without the rewards God will give to the faithful workers.

Verse 16: *Do you not know that you are a temple of God and that the Spirit of God dwells in you?*

After a slight digression (3:10-15) Paul returned to the thought of verse 9. His question was a mild rebuke. The right answer should have been common knowledge.[5] Paul used the plan of a typical Greek temple to pinpoint his goal. The word translated as **temple** refers to the dwelling place of God. **You** is plural. Christians as a community are God's dwelling place. Disunity was incompatible with God's presence.

Verse 17: *If any man destroys the temple of God, God will destroy him, for the temple of God is holy, and that is what you are.*

Disunity destroys the church. Therefore, to participate in divisions is to help destroy the dwelling place of God. Hence, those involved in this destruction face certain judgment.

Paul summarized his argument in 3:21-23. He prohibited the Corinthians from boasting about any man." Why did Paul prohibit the Corinthians' personal boasting? Paul's main point had to do with ownership. God owns all things. There is nothing the church can call its own. Christians themselves belong to God. He is the preeminent being of the universe. If the believers wanted to boast, let them boast about God.

Verse 21: *So then let no one boast in men. For all things belong to you,*

Christians should not idolize human leaders. If leaders are successful, God merits the credit. By limiting the party focus to a single servant of God, as the Corinthians were doing, they showed their enslavement to secular fashion. They had impoverished themselves, even though all of God's ministers were equally theirs.[6] Ministers (like Paul and Apollos) are God's gifts to His church.

Verse 22: *whether Paul or Apollos or Cephas or the world or life or death or things present or things to come; all things belong to you,*

By including all three Christian leaders, Paul made his point as comprehensive as possible. Paul piled up terms to emphasize to the Corinthians how comprehensive their possessions were. Because everything belongs to God, ***all things belong to*** God's people. Assets of material items and human leaders are the outcome of belonging to Christ by faith.

Verse 23: *and you belong to Christ; and Christ belongs to God.*

The church does not belong to any individual. Members do not own the church. Nor does the pastor and leaders possess the church. Christ is the Lord of the church. The church belongs to Him! Christ wields authority over the church, just as God has authority over Christ.

In chapter 4 Paul directed the Corinthians to consider him and Apollos as mere "servants of Christ" (4:1). Therefore, the apostle was accountable to Christ and so would be judged by Christ. He was confident that his future judgment would disclose his pure conscience. Paul encouraged the Christians at Corinth to consider him as an example they should follow. They should conclude from the harassment and hardship of Paul's ministry that their arrogant behavior revealed a flaw in their Christian character.

Paul promised to visit the church at Corinth. However, the members of that church would determine the nature of his visit. If they did not change, he would rebuke them. On the other hand, if they did change the visit would be loving and pleasant. It was their choice.

For Further Study

1. How can the divisions in the church at Corinth encourage today's adults to avoid divisiveness and focus on Christ?

2. Read about Apollos in the *Holman Bible Dictionary,* page 74, or in another Bible dictionary, or in "Apollos" in the Winter 1991 issue of the *Biblical Illustrator.*

3. Read "The Paradox of the Gospel" in the Winter 1992 issue of *Biblical Illustrator.*

4. Who are some Christians you know who have worked together with complementary assignments from God?

---

1 Otto Schmitz, παρακαλέω, παράκλησις, *Theological Dictionary of the New Testament,* 1967 ed., (Grand Rapids: Wm. B. Eerdmans Pub. Co., 1967), 5:774-76, 793-99.

2 Hans Conzelmann, *1 Corinthians: A Commentary on the First Epistle to the Corinthians,* trans. James W. Leitch, Hermeneia, ed. George W. Macrae (Philadelphia: Fortress Press, 1975), 35.

3 Raymond Bryan Brown, "1 Corinthians," *Broadman Bible Commentary* ed. Clifton J. Allen (Nashville: Broadman Press, 1970), vol. 10, 301 (hereinafter series cited as BBC).

4 Howard B. Foshee, *The Ministry of the Deacon* (Nashville: Convention Press, 1968), 17.

5 Leon Morris, *The First Epistle of Paul to the Corinthians: An Introduction and Commentary,* Tyndale New Testament Commentaries, ed. R. V. G. Tasker (n.p.: Tyndale Press, 1958), 69.

6 F. F. Bruce, *1 and 2 Corinthians,* New Century Bible, ed. Ronald E. Clements and Matthew Black (London: Marshall, Morgan, and Scott, 1971), 45-46.

June 8, 1997

Living Moral Lives

Background Passage: 1 Corinthians 5—6
Focal Passages: 1 Corinthians 5:1-5,9-13; 6:9-11

Introduction

We live in a culture saturated with sex. Erotic advertising is used to sell products of every description. The lyrics of many contemporary songs contain sexual innuendo. And family entertainment now implies that the sexual content is not graphic. This permissive attitude condones sexual immorality.

AIDS and other sexually transmitted diseases have lowered promiscuity. However, too often the stress of "safe sex" evades the consequence of immorality. Also, the tragic use of abortion for birth control has contributed to looser sexual morals. In today's terminology a monogamous relationship may mean simply one partner at a time. Ultimately, such limited strategy for addressing human sexual problems will not provide the best solutions. Sexual immorality is incompatible with faith in Christ. Christians should practice moral purity in their own lives. The church must not tolerate low standards of morality by its members.

1 Corinthians 5—6
1. Immorality in the Church (5:1-13)
2. Lawsuits Among Believers (6:1-8)
3. Sanctification Through Christ (6:9-20)

The Background

According to the Bible, God created people as sexual beings (Gen. 1:27). Human sexuality is an integral part of His design for a healthy individual. Sex may be part of God's design for humanity, but its role is tainted by sin. Such factors as biology, gender, emotions, behavior, attitudes, and values also influence sexual behavior. God's intention frequently is perverted.[1]

In the first century societal attitudes profoundly affected sexual conduct. The ancient Greeks believed that because the sexual urge was normal, it always should be appeased. As a result prostitution flourished so that men might gratify their most carnal urge.

The moral depravity of Corinth surpassed other cities. Sex within marriage was reserved for producing an heir. Pleasure was believed to come only from an individual who was not one's spouse, so infidelity was acceptable for both sexes. Women routinely gave one day a year to Aphrodite by serving as a prostitute in her temple. Paul brought the gospel to this corrupt environment. God's demand for moral purity quickly conflicted with the prevailing lifestyle. Christianity called for converts who previously never controlled sexual desires to a dramatic change from sexual immorality to sexual purity. The church at Corinth, however, was tolerating conduct by one of its members that even an immoral culture considered obscene.

The Lesson Passage

1. Immorality in the Church (5:1-13)

Paul moved to the most serious charge made by the people of Chloe. There was a moral problem in the church which required immediate correction.

Verse 1: *It is actually reported that there is immorality among you, and immorality of such a kind as does not exist even among the Gentiles, that someone has his father's wife.*

According to the Greek view of life, sexual intercourse, like eating and drinking, was a natural necessity. Men were permitted extra-marital sex. Homosexuality and prostitution were common, but excess and overindulgence were censured.

Roman society was beginning to restrain sexual promiscuity. Revelations that the orgies of Bacchus, the god of drink and drunkenness, were being used to cover up for crimes had forced the Roman Senate to virtually ban the public worship of that deity.[2] Stoic philosophy advocated fidelity.[3] Augustus made adultery a crime against the state. Most of the penalties applied primarily to women, but the effect curtailed extramarital affairs.[4] And Roman law forbade the type relationship described by Paul in verse 1! Even among depraved Corinthian unbelievers this situation was unspeakably shameful.

Chloe's people reported that **someone has his father's wife.** The exact meaning of this statement is debated. Modern readers are at a disadvantage because we only see Paul's part of the dialogue. The people at Corinth knew what the relationship was. Paul also knew, so he did not provide details in his letter. Incest was forbidden by Jewish law (Lev. 18:7-8; 20:11) and was punished by stoning. Thus incest does not seem to be the problem. The woman identified as his father's wife was apparently the man's step-mother.

Gentiles was the Jewish designation for those people outside Judaism. Here the term is used by Paul to designate those individuals outside the church. Thus he observed that the Corinthian pagans, who were without God, had a higher morality than did the people in the church at Corinth.

Verse 2: *You have become arrogant and have not mourned instead, so that the one who had done this deed would be removed from your midst.*

The Corinthian congregation had an attitude problem. They had **become arrogant.** Their pride allowed them to tolerate this most shocking sin, and they failed to rebuke the one who committed the transgression. They not only accepted his behavior, they took pride in it! However, Christ demands an unconditional repudiation of all extra-marital and unnatural sexual activity. Such behavior is sin; and its existence, especially in the church, should grieve believers.

Because the guilty person refused to correct his behavior, the church was under obligation to take action. The congregation should remove **the one who had done this deed** from their midst. He needed to be expelled from the church. His flagrant sinful conduct made genuine Christian fellowship with him impossible.

Often Christians refrain from condemnation. Frequently, they feel it is better to overlook the wrong than to offend the guilty person. If you had cancer, would you want your physician to ignore its presence because cancer is so unpleasant? Sin is even more harmful than cancer. Like any disease, it requires treatment. But any action by Christians should be taken in love.

Verse 3: *For I, on my part, though absent in body but present in spirit, have already judged him who has so committed this, as though I were present.*

Paul was in Ephesus, not Corinth. He could not talk to the Corinthians face to face. Although physically separated from the Corinthian church, Paul's interest in this situation united him to that congregation. He declared that he had already judged the person who committed the immoral act, as though he were present in Corinth. Paul may have intended that this statement remind the Corinthians of his apostolic authority.

Paul's attitude contrasted radically with that of the Corinthians. They were indifferent and cheerful. He was concerned and grieved. The *I* is emphatic. In substance, Paul said, "I know I am not present in Corinth, but you have made the wrong decision. I have made the correct decision. Now embrace my judgment and expel the man from the church!"

The guilty person may have been the same individual to whose punishment Paul referenced in 2 Corinthians 2:5-11. Regardless of the identification of the offender in this latter passage, it is instructive for handling church discipline. The goal of church discipline is redemptive, not punitive. Once the guilty party acknowledges wrongdoing and seeks forgiveness, the disciplinary action should be terminated.

Verse 4: *In the name of our Lord Jesus, when you are assembled, and I with you in spirit, with the power of our Lord Jesus,*

In the Scriptures **name** usually represents the character of the one bearing it. Thus the **name of our Lord Jesus** implies that any action by the church must conform to the character of Christ as revealed in these names. The title **Lord** identifies Christ with the God of the Old Testament. God said His name means, "I AM WHO I AM" (Ex. 3:13-14). At least one implication of this divine revelation is that God's nature does not change. Jesus is the eternal, unchanging Deity. The name *Jesus* is the Greek form of the Hebrew name *Joshua*. It means "The Lord is salvation," or "The Lord saves." Thus church discipline must conform to the nature of the God who consistently acts to save humanity from sin! Church discipline has redemptive purposes. It should deliver guilty people from their sinful behavior and preserve the message of the gospel as presented by the church.

Church discipline is not an individual action. It only should be conducted by the entire church body when they have gathered together for that purpose. Paul had expressed the opinion that this man should be removed from the church. The apostle did not consider his words to be personal. Rather, he regarded himself as the leader of the assembly. The facts established the man's guilt. His situation was irreconcilable to the gospel. Now the assembly needed only to pass sentence. Paul's **and I with you in spirit** indicated that he shared responsibility for the action.

Church discipline is not for revenge. It must be done in the **name of our Lord Jesus** and **with the power of our Lord Jesus.** Action not only must conform to Christ's nature, it must result from the empowerment of Christ. The Lordship of Christ should control the proceedings.

Verse 5: *I have decided to deliver such a one to Satan for the destruction of his flesh, so that his spirit may be saved in the day of the Lord Jesus.*

Paul had decided **to deliver** this immoral church member **to Satan for the destruction of his flesh.** Two ideas seem to be present in Paul's statement. The offender was to be excommunicated from the church, and he would suffer some physical harm. The logic behind this unusual phrase recognized that the church submitted to the Lordship of Christ. Outside the church was the sphere of Satan. Satan's realm had not yet been placed in subjugation to Christ. Thus, the offending member was to be put into the domain where Satan ruled. **The destruction of his flesh** may either refer to physical death or to purging of the sin-centered way of life.

Whatever the specific action Paul demanded, its purpose was *that his spirit may be saved*. Because "flesh" is placed in opposition to "spirit," flesh seems to refer to the man's physical body. Thus Paul hoped that physical suffering might cause the man to repent. *The day of the Lord* was that occasion predicted by the prophets when God would intervene in human history. At that time God would punish evil-doers and reward the righteous. Paul's addition of the personal name *Jesus* denoted that the punishment of evildoers would take place upon the return of Christ. Thus, while the man's physical body might be destroyed, he would be saved at the second coming of Christ.

As a method for illustrating his point, Paul cited the traditional removal of leaven from the Jewish home before Passover (5:6-8). This illustration may suggest that 1 Corinthians was written near Passover. Leaven represented evil in the Jewish world of the first century A.D. Here Paul portrays the Passover lamb as already having been slain, but all of the leaven had not been cleaned out of the house. Such a predicament was an impossible situation. The leaven needed to be removed without delay. Otherwise, the Passover meal could not be eaten as long as evil resided in the house.

Verse 9: *I wrote you in my letter not to associate with immoral people;*

The Book of 1 Corinthians was actually the second letter Paul wrote concerning the problems in Corinth (see introductory article). In a previous letter he had advised the Corinthian Christians **not to associate with immoral people.** The Corinthian church apparently misunderstood Paul's instructions. Therefore, Paul sought to correct their misconception about his former directives.

Verse 10: *I did not at all mean with the immoral people of this world, or with the covetous and swindlers, or with idolaters, for then you would have to go out of the world.*

Paul added other categories of sinners to the **immoral people of this world.** Sin is sin. While Paul was addressing a specific situation, he did not propose to isolate sexual sins from other evil conduct.

Covetous literally means the one "who must have more." Here it has the sense of "striving for material possessions." The word **swindlers** refers to one who takes something forcefully.[5] Because of the violence involved in taking something by force, the English word **swindlers** may not clearly convey that violence. These two groups should be taken together. The former seized the property of others by cunning. The latter seized property by violence. **Idolaters** are those who have a wrong relationship with God. They worship false deities and allow these imitation gods to control their lives.

If Paul had meant that contact with all sinners was to stop, then Christians could not live in human society. **They would have to go out** *of the world.* In the notoriously immoral environment of Corinth, a literal application of Paul's previous letter would have resulted in no contact with some family members, business associates, and social acquaintances. Paul's language asserted that such an idea contradicted Christ's revealed will for His followers. During the night before His crucifixion, Jesus prayed that His disciples might remain in the world but not be of the world (John 17:15-16,18). One who isolates himself or herself from the world cannot be an effective witness to the world.

Verse 11: *But actually, I wrote to you not to associate with any so-called brother if he is an immoral person, or covetous, or an idolater, or a reviler, or a drunkard, or a swindler—not even to eat with such a one.*

Paul warned the Corinthian church not to tolerate such immorality among its members. He enumerated a list of flagrant sins, which so contradicted the purpose of church membership that anyone practicing them should be isolated. Other Christians were **not even to eat with such a one.** The separation between Christians seeking to do what is right and Christians who take the name of Christ but not the lifestyle of Christ is absolute.

Verse 12: *For what have I to do with judging outsiders? Do you not judge those who are within the church?*

What is the Christian's attitude toward individuals who are blatant sinners? To involve the believers in forming the correct view, the apostle asked two rhetorical questions. The obvious answer to his first question is" nothing." Paul made it clear that a believer is not to act as a judge of non-believers. But the second question expects a yes answer. It is the church's duty to judge its members. The church has a responsibility to maintain certain standards. Morally hardened and corrupt members need to be corrected.

Verse 13: *But those who are outside, God judges. Remove the wicked man from among yourselves.*

The judgment of those outside the church must be left to God. By expelling immoral members from the church, the church removes them from church jurisdiction and so leaves them to God's judgment. They become outsiders.

2. Lawsuits Among Unbelievers (6:1-8)

Perhaps someone suggested that because the immorality previously described was illegal, the offender should be taken to court. Paul objected. He did accept the justice of the Roman legal system. On occasion Paul appealed for his own legal rights as a Roman citizen (Acts 16:37; 22:25; 25:10-11). But Roman courts were totally pagan, and the church should not bring its internal disputes before pagans.

Christianity was a new religion with moral values similar to Judaism. Few Gentiles, however, knew much about Judaism. Most Romans regarded Jews as superstitious. They misunderstood the Sabbath observance as an excuse for idleness. The Jewish division of humanity into Jews and Gentiles was greatly resented.[6] Paul believed Christians' taking one another to court was inappropriate in such an environment. They could not be effective witnesses for Christ by declaring a faith founded on love and then filing lawsuits against other Christians.

Paul argued that Christians were competent to settle disputes without resorting to the courts. Because of our relationship to Christ, Christians will be associated with Him in the final judgment. We even will participate in the judgment of the angels. The term *angel* denotes a type of created being. While the term normally is associated with loyal servants of God, Satan and his demons are from the angelic order.

Arguing from a greater to a lesser case, Paul concluded that if Christians are capable of judging the world, then surely they can settle less significant cases. Regardless of a court's verdict, the existence of lawsuits between believers actually means that both parties are losers. It is better for a believer to be wronged than to hurt another believer.

3. Sanctification Through Christ (6:9-20)

Having discredited the notion of legal action, Paul returned to the problem of immorality and the larger problem of sin in the church. The activities cataloged by Paul were not isolated acts but a way of life. Such deeds are incompatible with Christianity.

Verses 9-10: *Or do you not know that the unrighteous will not inherit the kingdom of God? Do not be deceived; neither fornicators, nor idolaters, nor adulterers, nor effeminate, nor homosexuals, 10 nor thieves, nor the covetous, nor drunkards, nor revilers, nor swindlers, will inherit the kingdom of God.*

The stress of the term **unrighteous** is on the character of those described, not the group as a class. To think of the gospel as an effort to reform society is a major error. The non-Christian will not put into practice the ethics of Christ. A fundamental transformation of a person's character is required. The unrighteous are those individuals whose lifestyles reveal that they are not right with God.

During the Old Testament era, the **kingdom of God** was a future hope that one day God would act to establish His sovereign rule over humanity. In the Person and work of Christ, the kingdom of God entered into the world. In the lives of believers, the kingdom is a present reality, not only a future hope. Christ is Lord.

Paul did not suggest that those guilty of sinful behavior cannot repent and receive God's forgiveness. But he warned **Do not be de-**

ceived. Continuation in a lifestyle characterized by any of the sins listed indicates that Christ has not established His sovereignty over that individual. Before their conversion such behavior had been customary for many believers, but salvation transformed them into a new creation. The past lifestyle was exchanged for the goal of becoming like Christ. Now the old behavior is inadmissible.

Fornication is a general term for sexual activity outside of marriage. Extramarital sex was commonplace in the Gentile world, but God condemned it. The occurrence of *idolaters* in a list of sexual evils seems out of place. However, the misuse of sex inevitably leads to a perversion of the Creator and to the elevation of creation to God's level, which is idolatry. *Adulterers* violate the Seventh Commandment (Ex. 20:14; Deut. 5:18). The word *effeminate* is a synonym for "sickness."[7] It basically means soft. The term may allude to passive and active homosexuals.[8] Or it may refer to male prostitutes.[9] In classical Greece homosexual activity, primarily among men, was typical behavior. By the Roman Era not only was male homosexuality still popular, lesbian liaisons had become fashionable. But the lifestyle *of homosexuals* was and is unacceptable to God.

The Eighth Commandment forbids stealing (Ex. 20:15; Deut. 5:19). Covetousness violates the Tenth Commandment (Ex. 20:17; Deut. 5:21). An addiction to some type of drug elevates that substance to the status of deity in the addict's life. Alcohol was the most common drug of choice in the first-century Roman world. Routinely, it was abused. *Revilers* are people who abuse other people.

Verse 11: *Such were some of you; but you were washed, but you were sanctified, but you were justified in the name of the Lord Jesus Christ and in the Spirit of our God.*

The sins previously listed also were characteristic of many believers' preconversion lifestyles, but Jesus Christ had changed them. These sins were past history, not present activity. The Corinthians **were washed,** spiritually cleansed by God, an act symbolized in the ordinance of baptism. **Sanctified** means "to set apart" and refers to God's action of making a sinner a saint. The dominant idea of sanctification is separation from from sin and separation to a sacred purpose. **Justified** is a legal term meaning to declare righteous. The word occurs four times in these two verses. When God justifies a sinner, He declares that person righteous because of his or her faith in Christ and only because of faith in Christ. All three actions (washed, sanctified, justified) occurred when the Corinthians believed the gospel.

Some of the Corinthian Christians had been living the pagan lifestyle that Paul described in verses 9-10. However, a great change had taken place in their lives. They had become new people. They had been purified from sin's defilement. They had been set apart to holy living.

They had been put right with God. None of this major change had been their achievement. Rather, it had been God's gift to them.

In view of the changes that had been accomplished in their lives by Christ, they now were in His possession. They were also indwelt by God's Spirit. Because they have a new existence, they must live in the power of that new existence. They must be controlled by the Holy Spirit instead of by any other substance or false god.

For Further Study

1. Read about Passover in the *Holman Bible Dictionary* article on festivals, pages 484-490, or in another Bible dictionary.

2. Read about Paul's contacts with Corinth during his Ephesian ministry in the *Holman Bible Dictionary* article on 1 Corinthians, pages 301-302, or in another Bible dictionary.

3. What guidelines should adults use to determine if it is proper to pass judgment on other individuals?

---

1 Jack O. Balswick and Judith K. Balswick, *The Family: A Christian Perspective on the Contemporary Home* (Grand Rapids: Baker Book House, 1991), 171.

2 Reay Tannahill, *Sex in History* (New York: Stein and Day, 1980), 118-19.

3 Glen McCoy, "Prostitution in the First Century," *Biblical Illustrator* 17 (Fall 1991): 37-38.

4 Tannahill, *Sex in History,* p. 123.

5 Werner Foerster, ἁρπάζω, ἁρπαγμός, *Theological Dictionary of the New Testament,* (Grand Rapids: Wm. B. Eerdmans Pub. Co., 1967), 1:472.

6 J. P. V. D. Balsdon, *Romans and Aliens* (Chapel Hill, North Carolina: University of North Carolina Press, 1979), 67.

7 A. Oepke, νόσος, νοσέω, νόσημα (μαλακία, μάστιζ, κακῶς ἔχω), *Theological Dictionary of the New Testament,* (Grand Rapids: Wm. B. Eerdmans Pub. Co., 1967), 4:1091.

8 Brown, "1 Corinthians," *Broadman Bible Commentary,* vol. 10, 323.

9 Mare, "1 Corinthians," *Expositor's Bible Commentary* (Grand Rapids, Michigan: Zondervan, 1976), vol. 10, 223.

June 15, 1997

Being Faithful in Marriage

Background Passage 1 Corinthians 7
Focal Passages: 1 Corinthians 7:1-16

Introduction

The newspaper headline caught my attention: "D-I-V-O-R-C-E, The culture of divorce has failed to deliver on its promise of individual happiness." The article lamented the attitude that viewed marriage as an institution only "as long as I'm happy." It noted that no consensus of opinion exists concerning the precise relationship of society's problems to the dissolution of the family. Yet, many agree that marriage no longer has the same value as it had 50 years ago. The author concluded that the moral worth of marriage needs to be reintroduced into our culture.[1]

Questions concerning singleness, marriage, and divorce are common. The responses given by the secular world have failed to yield satisfactory results. The Scriptures provide solid answers. God approves of both singleness and marriage. Each person is accountable for being faithful to God and if married to his or her spouse.

1 Corinthians 7
1. Advantages of Being Married (7:1-9)
2. Advice About Staying Married (7:10-16)
3. Present Circumstances and God's Will (7:17-24)
4. Advantages of Being Single (7:25-40)

The Background

By the first century A.D. women in the Roman world were exerting a fresh independence. They owned property and reclined at dinner in the same fashion as men.[2] Marriage reflected their new status. Childbearing and housekeeping were now only part of a wife's role. She participated in the business of the family. Marriage was strictly monogamous, but divorce was common. Under Roman law a person could divorce a spouse for virtually no reason. Grounds for separation included the rise of the husband to a higher social class, a barren wife, or the desire to marry someone else. Divorce proceedings were simple and straightforward; only an official notification was required.[3] The necessity to divide property was the major restraining influence against divorce in Roman times.[4]

Among the Corinthian believers marriage was esteemed lightly, but some Christians presumably advocated celibacy. They even may have suggested that marriage indicated spiritual immaturity. Whatever the specific issue relating to marriage and celibacy, the believers wrote Paul for his judgment. Thus in these verses the apostle was answering their question, not recommending one status over the other.

The Lesson Passage

1. Advantages of Being Married (7:1-9)

Verse 1: *Now concerning the things about which you wrote, it is good for a man not to touch a woman.*

The exact content of **the things about which you wrote** is not known. The content suggests that the Corinthians may have asked if *it is good for a man to touch a woman?* Undoubtedly, the inquiry concerned celibacy and marriage. Paul seemed to prefer being single over being married (see v. 8). However, his preference was because of the "present distress" (v. 26). This distress was a local situation, and its nature is a mystery. The distress could have been an external persecution, but there is no record the Corinthians were suffering persecution at that time. Or it might have been the church's attitude towards marriage, but seems to have been more general. Whatever the exact nature was, the distress was not an ordinary event. Elsewhere in the New Testament, Paul wrote of the virtue of marriage (Col. 3:18-19; 1 Tim. 3:2,12). Sometimes being single may be preferable to marriage. At other times it is more appropriate to marry.

Verse 2: *But because of immoralities, each man is to have his own wife, and each woman is to have her own husband.*

While celibacy is good, few individuals want to live without sexual relations. The reference to **each man** and to **each woman** indicates that both desire sex. God created humanity with a sex drive. His first command to humankind was to "be fruitful and multiply" (Gen. 1:28). Obedience to His command cannot take place without procreation. Sex is a gift from God, but promiscuity is abhorrent to God. Therefore, most people should marry.

The marriage relationship is an exclusive union. A man should have **his own wife,** and a woman should have **her own husband.** Male and female were created to complement each other physically and emotionally. In marriage they establish a completeness, which the Bible refers to as "one flesh" (Gen. 2:24). That oneness can only be accomplished through an exclusive and permanent relationship. Anything other than an exclusive and permanent relationship destroys the oneness that God intended to be maintained between a man and a woman.

Verses 3-4: *The husband must fulfill his duty to his wife, and likewise also the wife to her husband. 4 The wife does not have authority over her own body, but the husband does; and likewise also the husband does not have authority over his own body, but the wife does.*

Marriage is a commitment into which both the man and the woman mutually and freely enter. Each party embraces the other as his or her own unique companion, and each submits to the needs of the other. Thus husband and wife relinquish personal privileges to satisfy the spouse. In the sexual relationship such commitment becomes a mutual responsibility.

Self-gratification is not the objective; rather, each one aspires to satisfy the other one. The expression "Not tonight, I have a headache" has become an idiom for "I don't want to have sex tonight." This attitude is selfish. The biblical mandate is the opposite of this popular idea. In Christian marriage both husband and wife have a **duty** to respond to the sexual advances of their partner. Sex is frequently called the language of love. Christians certainly can express the biblical idea of love in marriage. Each time they freely put the needs of their spouse ahead of their own, they say, "I love you."

Verse 5: *Stop depriving one another, except by agreement for a time, so that you may devote yourselves to prayer, and come together again so that Satan will not tempt you because of your lack of self-control.*

Paul placed conditions on sexual abstinence by married couples. Abstinence should only occur by mutual agreement and be for a spiritual purpose. It is not a permanent state but is for a limited period. During abstinence from sexual relations, the couple should **devote** themselves **to prayer.** Such behavior is appropriate during a spiritual crisis or when making important decisions. However, the time of abstinence should be brief. Otherwise, **Satan** will take advantage of the sex drive and **tempt** Christians to commit adultery. Temptation can quickly induce a believer to sin. Then the result of mutually agreed abstinence will be the opposite of its intention.

Verse 6: *But this I say by way of concession, not of command.*

I say by way of concession simply means this was Paul's opinion. The apostle distinguished his own conclusions from those truths taught to him by others. In verse 10 Paul's statement "not I, but the Lord" indicates that his instructions about marriage came from the teaching ministry of Jesus. Paul knew precisely what Jesus had said on that topic, so Paul cited the Lord. Christ, however, did not address the issue of celibacy verses marriage. Therefore, in this verse (v. 6) Paul refused to equate his belief with a divine command. Rather, he drew a conclusion based on his own understanding of Christ's teachings. This does not mean Paul's conclusion is invalid; rather, his conclusion is a part of the Scripture and has the same authority as any Scripture passage. Paul's point is based on its inspiration by the Holy Spirit. Later, Paul expressed to the Corinthians his evaluation of his judgment when he stated, "I think that I also have the Spirit of God" (7:40).

This verse may refer only to the previous verse. If so, Paul was saying that his conditions for sexual abstinence were practical advice, not rigid commandments. Or the verse may relate to the entire discussion on marriage and celibacy. In that verse Paul was indicating that marriage or celibacy was a personal choice, and that one's choice does not make one a lesser Christian.

Verse 7: *Yet I wish that all men were even as I myself am. However, each man has his own gift from God, one in this manner, and another in that.*

Paul perceived that celibacy had certain advantages. Celibacy allows one to serve God without distraction. It was Paul's preference for himself. Nonetheless, he realized that advocating celibacy was impractical. Furthermore, Paul understood that for some individuals celibacy was wrong. Their need for marriage did not reflect a flaw in their Christian character. Rather, it was the consequence of God's **gift** to that person.

God had called Paul to be an itinerant missionary. The length of his stay in one location varied from a few days to three years. Marriage would have hindered his ministry. So God gifted him with an ability to live without marriage. Yet Paul recognized that God gifted others in a different manner. Peter maintained a home in Capernaum even after he followed Jesus, (Matt. 8:14). When Peter became a prominent leader of the church, his wife traveled with him (1 Cor. 9:5). Paul was wise enough to understand that the difference between his marital status and that of Peter was God's provision for each man.

Verses 8-9: *But I say to the unmarried and to widows that it is good for them if they remain even as I. 9 But if they do not have self-control, let them marry; for it is better to marry than to burn with passion.*

Paul was single. However, no evidence exists to determine if he was a widower or had never been married. **Good** means that it is all right for the unmarried and those who are widowed to remain single. The word does not imply that it would be bad if they decided to marry. While Paul encouraged others to remain single, he recognized that some could not cope with the chaste lifestyle. So he observed that it was **better to marry than to burn** with sexual desire.

2. Advice About Staying Married (7:10-16)

Verse 10: *But to the married I give instructions, not I, but the Lord, that the wife should not leave her husband*

Paul turned his attention to married couples who were Christians. He no longer stated his opinion only. Jesus had spoken specifically concerning divorce (Matt. 5:31-32; 19:3-12; Mark 10:2-12; Luke 16:18). Therefore, the apostle wrote **But to the married I give instructions, not I, but the Lord.** The absence of any reference to unchastity suggests that even adultery should not necessitate divorce. God restored Hosea's marriage even after the glaring infidelity and idolatry of Gomer (Hos. 1—3). If both partners will look to God's grace, any obstacle to continued matrimony can be overcome. Christians should not initiate separation or divorce. For the unmarried to remain single is "good," but for the married to remain married is the revealed will of Jesus Christ.

Verse 11: *(but if she does leave, she must remain unmarried, or else be reconciled to her husband), and that the husband should not divorce his wife.*

Although continuation of a marriage is preferable, reality is that separation does occur. If a marriage was dissolved, Paul warned the Corinthians that they should not compound their error with another marriage. When a believer is separated, it is best to be reconciled or remain single. The language of the wife leaving (v. 10) and the husband sending his wife away reflects the legal status of men and women in the Roman world. The essence of Paul's comments is that both husband and wife have responsibility for preservation of the marriage. A Christian couple should resolve to work out problems and maintain their marriage.

Verses 12-13: *But to the rest I say, not the Lord, that if any brother has a wife who is an unbeliever, and she consents to live with him, he must not divorce her. 13 And a woman who has an unbelieving husband, and he consents to live with her, she must not send her husband away.*

Paul next dealt with the case of a non-Christian married couple. The background of verse 12 probably was that after the wedding one spouse was converted. The differences between an unbeliever and a believer caused a rift in the union. Should the two continue to live as husband and wife? Jesus never addressed this specific issue. Therefore, Paul wrote **I say, not the Lord.** Based on his understanding of Christ, the gospel, and marriage Paul reached the decision that if the unbeliever consented to live together the Christian was obligated to continue in the marriage. The determination of separation or divorce was the unbeliever's choice.

Verse 14: *For the unbelieving husband is sanctified through his wife, and the unbelieving wife is sanctified through her believing husband; for otherwise your children are unclean, but now they are holy.*

The exact sense in which an unbelieving spouse is **sanctified** is widely debated. Clearly, Paul did not imply that salvation can be mediated through marriage (v. 16). Salvation can only come by faith in the Lord Jesus Christ (Eph. 2:8-9). Perhaps the best explanation of the word *sanctified* in this verse is that one spouse can create a godly atmosphere in the home. This atmosphere moves the lost mate closer to God through godly influence and exposure to truth. Likewise, one devout parent can provide a better environment in which to rear children than two unbelievers. Without the presence of the believing spouse, the children would grow up in a totally pagan home.

In the Old Testament "unclean," "clean," and "holy" denoted a person's or object's usefulness to God. "Clean" was the state where something was normal and so useful to people. "Holy" designated that which was set apart for use by God. "Unclean" meant that the person or object was of no benefit to either people or God.

For example, clean sheep produced wool or provided food. A holy lamb was without defect and designated by its owner as a sacrifice in worship. But disease or deformity made a sheep unclean; thus, it was considered to be useless. The sheep neither provided wool nor food nor sacrifice.

Children with a Christian parent are holy only in the sense they have been taught about God and therefore are closer to a state of usefulness to Him. In contrast, children of unbelievers have no knowledge of or experience with God. Therefore, they can be of little service to Him. If these latter children learn of God and trust Him, they too can become useful to His service.

One of the most difficult places to exhibit Christian character can be in our own home. We tend to lower our guard in our home, but temptation stalks us even there. Before we even realize it, we have said or done something we regret. Our Christian influence can have the greatest impact at home. Our family is watching us. They see us living out our faith on a daily basis. What a spouse and children observe may sway them to accept or to reject Christ.

Verse 15: *Yet if the unbelieving one leaves, let him leave; the brother or the sister is not under bondage in such cases, but God has called us to peace.*

Paul always left the decision for terminating the marriage to the unbeliever. The Christian should not initiate the separation. If the unbeliever dissolves the relationship, however, the believer no longer is obligated to the terms of the marriage covenant. The phrase **God has called us to peace** may apply to the entire issue of marriages between

Christians and unbelievers. In this case the idea is that a believer should make every effort to maintain harmony at home. If the phrase only applies to the previous clause (**the brother or sister is not under bondage in such cases**), then the idea is that the believer should not force the discontented partner to remain in the union.

Verse 16: *For how do you know, O wife, whether you will save your husband? Or how do you know, O husband, whether you will save your wife?*

These questions may be intended to comfort the believer whose spouse has left. One does not know if the spouse would have been saved if the marriage lasted. So the rejected partner should not feel guilt or engage in unprofitable speculation. Or the questions may imply that the believer should stay with the unbelieving spouse in the hope the non-Christian will be saved. Or probably both connotations are present. Because the decision of divorce belonged to the non-Christian, the Christian is not responsible for its consequences. And if the non-Christian elects to stay, hope for that individual's salvation remains. Remember that Paul was talking about the situation where one member of a non-Christian couple converts to the faith. He was not talking about a Christian deliberately marrying a non-Christian. **Save** here refers to salvation from sin, not to salvaging the marriage relationship. The verse does not suggest that a spouse can actually save another spouse. Rather, as has been previously stated, the Christian's influence brings the lost spouse to trust Christ as savior.

3. Present Circumstances and God's Will (7:17-24)

Paul discussed circumstances, not job assignments. One's calling is to be a Christian. A Christian is to maintain the fullest Christian character regardless of what happens. The Christian is to be faithful to Christ in every circumstance. Rituals that distinguish religious groups do not help one to live a Christian life. Obeying God is what counts. Nor should the Christian be ruled by an economic state or social status. A Christian in slavery could use the bondage as an occasion to witness. But if presented with the opportunity for freedom, he or she could take advantage of the circumstance. Christians belong to God and are all equal in Christ. Therefore, Christians should be content in any circumstance, knowing God has placed them there for some divine purpose.

4. Advantages of Being Single (7:25-40)

Paul's statement about virgins (v. 25) was made in direct response to a question raised by the Corinthians. Like the other questions answered in this letter, the specific question the Corinthians had asked Paul no longer is known. At that time all decisions about marriage were made by parents or guardians, not the individual. So this section may be primarily advice to Christian fathers concerning arrangements for their daughters. As he wrote, Paul interjected comments about the advantages of being single and the responsibilities of marriage.

Is Paul's advice in verse 26 a general truth for all time or an application to a specific situation? Would Paul have written these words without the "present distress?" If it is a general truth for all time, then marriage for Christians would be wrong. At best it would imply that married couples are less spiritual than singles. If it is an application to a specific situation, then the principle is that there are times when, because of the circumstance, it is better not to marry. The former does not harmonize with other Scriptures. The latter does. Therefore, clearly the latter interpretation is preferable.

Paul's words can be paraphrased: "My real interest is that you are not overly concerned because of the present local trouble. I want your mind freed from temporal things so you can focus on spiritual." The "present distress" was a temporary event particular to the situation at Corinth. So these verses must be interpreted in the context of some external circumstance. These verses do not imply Paul disliked women. Rather, he understood that families create responsibilities. Later, Paul wrote to Timothy that one who failed to provide for his own family denied the faith and was worse than an unbeliever (1 Tim. 5:8). Because of the local situation in Corinth, it was better not to have family obligations at that time.

According to one point of view, verses 36-38 refer to a husband and wife who are living without sexual intercourse. Thus, they are free to consummate the union. Others presume they were an engaged couple. They are told that if they can control their physical passion, they should remain single. But if they cannot, by all means marry! However, the best interpretation is that verses 36-38 were written to a father about his daughter. The italic print indicates that the word *daughter* does not occur in the Greek text. Something Paul had written previously had kept a father from securing a husband for his daughter. The daughter was "full of age," or literally in her "prime." According to Plato, she would be 20 years of age.[5] Again, these verses were an answer to a question or situation in Corinth. It implies that someone had refused to allow his daughter to marry. The church had asked if the father could do that. Paul responded that the father could do what he wanted and be right either way.

Paul closed his discussion on marriage with counsel to widows. He stressed the permanence of marriage. Marriage is a lifelong commitment and rarely is divorce warranted. But the death of one spouse terminates the marriage restrictions. The surviving spouse is free to remarry. However, because of the local situation, Paul advised the widows of Corinth to remain single.

For Further Study

1. Read "Divorce According to Ancient -Roman Law" in the Fall 1991 issue of the *Biblical Illustrator.*
2. Read about marriage in the *Holman Bible Dictionary,* pages 924-27, or in another Bible dictionary.
3. How should Christian adults view sexual union within the total context of a marriage relationship?
4. What are some specific situations in which being single is a distinct advantage? What are some other situations in which it is better to be married? Why do you feel this way?

---

1 *The Columbus, Georgia, Ledger-Enquirer* (Monday, April 17, 1995), see. a, 6.

2 Michael Grant, *History of Rome* (New York: Charles Scribner's Sons, 1978), 243-44.

3 Gerald Stephens, "Divorce According to Ancient Graeco-Roman Law, *Biblical Illustrator* 17 (Fall 1991): 53-54; Tannahill, Sex in History, 122; Albrecht Oepke, "γυνή," *Theological Dictionary of the New Testament,* (Grand Rapids: Wm. B. Eerdmans Pub. Co., 1964), 1:777-80.

4 Tannahill, "Sex in History" 122.

5 Leon Morris, *The First Epistle of Paul to the Corinthians,* Tyndale New Testament Commentaries, 120.

June 22, 1997

Tempering Freedom with Love

Background Passage: 1 Corinthians 8
Focal Passage: 1 Corinthians 8:1-13

Introduction

The State Department of Natural Resources had implanted more than 40,000 largemouth bass with tiny electronic devices to track their growth and movement. The devices were placed under the skin of the fish and therefore were not visible. The fish were then released in the nearby river. When signals came from the ponds of a local fish farm, the authorities investigated. They arrested the owner of the farm, and the fishermen who sold him the wiretapped fish. A black-market ring that illegally sold more than 40,000 pounds of game fish was put out of business.[1] For these culprits the bass caught in the river came with unexpected consequences.

Most wrong actions come with unexpected consequences. Often these consequences involve how others perceive us and our actions. Sometimes these unexpected results are positive. At other times they are negative.

Immature Christians sometimes misunderstand certain activities done by more mature believers. As a result the behavior of strong believers can actually lead weaker believers into sin. Therefore, mature Christians need to be conscientious about what they say or do. Love is more important than their knowledge and freedom. Christian love dictates that strong believers do not damage the faith of weaker Christians or induce them to do wrong.

1 Corinthians 8
1. Love Superior to Knowledge (8:1-3)
2. God Superior to Idols (8:4-6)
3. Influence Superior to Freedom (8:7-13)

The Background

Either in their letter to Paul or through the delegation from Chloe, the Corinthians had asked if it was sinful to eat meat sacrificed to the idols of pagan gods. Animal sacrifice was universal in the ancient world. It was the primary means for approaching the deity of every religion. The sacrifice was an expression of worship and devotion. It was an integral part, not only of religion, but of the culture in every city.

Most social functions involved banquets. Those banquets served meat that usually had been previously sacrificed to false gods. Refusal to eat meat sacrificed to idols could result in complete separation from family and society.

Many sacrifices required only a portion of the animal be burnt on the altar. The remaining meat was given to the priests or returned to the worshiper to use. Wealthy citizens in Corinth customarily took the meat from their sacrifices and held banquets. In addition, major social events for the community often were held in the temples of pagan gods. The meat served at these festivities came from sacrifices at the temple. Poor inhabitants sold their leftover meat to the city's butchers to sell in the market. Whenever the priests had more meat than they could consume, they likewise sold the surplus to the butchers. Indeed, much of the meat bought and sold in the public markets of Corinth was from animals sacrificed to the idols in its temples.

Unwillingness to eat such meat might result in social isolation or the loss of meat in one's diet. Thus, the question about the suitability of eating meat sacrificed to idols was not a hypothetical inquiry. For the Corinthians the answer had real significance for their daily lives. Physical health, emotional well-being, and spiritual vitality were affected by the answer.

The Lesson Passage

1. Love Superior to Knowledge (8:1-3)

A knowledge of Jesus Christ is the important element in faith. An experience with Christ implants a personal knowledge of God in the heart and mind of an individual. Knowledge should produce a deeper insight into God's will and conformity to His will. But knowledge can cause individuals to claim to be more spiritual than others. Such pride is erroneous and contrary to the truth of the gospel. Pride is built on what people think they have accomplished by themselves. Thus pride has no place in a relationship that a person has not worked to make but has received from God.

Verse 1: *Now concerning things sacrificed to idols, we know that we all have knowledge. Knowledge makes arrogant, but love edifies.*

At this point in his letter, Paul responded to the inquiry **concerning things sacrificed to idols.** He began by conceding that all of his readers had some degree of understanding about the issue. **We all have knowl-**

edge, may be a quotation from the believers' letter to Paul. Presumably, everyone agreed that the gods represented by the idols were imaginary. Apparently, however, some members of the church were puffed up in their knowledge. Paul struck at their intellectual pride. Knowledge can make individuals think they are what they ought to be. They then become arrogant, believing themselves superior to other church members. On the other hand, love edifies. Love makes people be what they should be. Christian love is selfless. It is attentive solely with the object of the love.

God's love secured our salvation. Sinners are transformed into saints by love. As love operates within the life of the believer, the Christian seeks to serve unselfishly the needs of others.

Verse 2: *If anyone supposes that he knows anything, he has not yet known as he ought to know;*

The Corinthians were enamored with knowledge. Certain ones of them took great pride in the fact that they were more knowledgeable than other church members. Paul reminded them that human knowledge is incomplete. Truly intelligent individuals recognize that their ignorance is far greater than their knowledge. Realizing one lacks knowledge is the first step in acquiring knowledge. The conviction that one has acquired sufficient knowledge means the individual has not yet gained the most basic knowledge. To think, "I do not need to know any more," is a drastic mistake.

Verse 3: *but if anyone loves God, he is known by Him.*

Love based on faith is the key to a personal relationship with God. Jesus said the first and most important commandment in the Old Testament is that we love the Lord our God with our entire being (Matt. 22:37-38). God does not enter into a relationship with people because they know certain facts about Him. Even the demons know certain facts about God, and their knowledge causes them to shudder in fear (Jas. 2:19). Their knowledge about God, however, does not transform them into angels. God enters into covenant with those who respond to His love by trusting Him.

God understands the most confidential details about us. He is intimately aware of our sin. Yet because Christ loves us, He still died for us. He did so because of God's love (John 3:16). Our salvation is rooted in God's love for us. To be known by Him is the same as being in personal union with God.

2. God Superior to Idols (8:4-6)

Idolatry was typical of most religions in the ancient world, but Israel was unique in its prohibition of images and icons. The New Testament writers expanded the definition of idolatry to include the worship of false gods, not just the use of an idol. False gods are manufactured in the imagination of sinful humanity. In these verses Paul employed the word *idol* in this wider sense. The word designated all false gods. The designation marked them as objects, recognized they were not divine, and declared they were in fact nothing. Idols have no real existence. Since idols are nothing, they can have no influence on life.

Verse 4: *Therefore concerning the eating of things sacrificed to idols, we know that there is no such thing as an idol in the world, and that there is no God but one.*

Therefore indicates the discussion that follows is connected to the previous argument. Having asserted that the Christian's relationship with God is based on love, Paul returned to the topic of **eating of things sacrificed to idols.** Earlier he conceded that all his readers shared some knowledge on the subject (v. 1). At this point Paul identified specifically the knowledge on which everyone agreed. People called idols gods, but an idol was not a real deity. It was an object made of wood, stone, silver, or gold. These inanimate objects were incapable of receiving the sacrifices offered to them. There was **but one** true and living God.

The fundamental tenet of ancient Judaism was monotheism, the belief in only one **God** (Isa. 44:6; 45:5). This belief separated Israel's religion from those of its neighbors. Christianity persisted in this uncommon belief. God is one, but He reveals Himself as Father, Son, and Holy Spirit but without division of His being. The doctrine of the Trinity may be impossible to comprehend, but it does not tolerate polytheism. Only non-Christians believe in other gods.

Verses 5-6: *For even if there are so-called gods whether in heaven or on earth, as indeed there are many gods and many lords,* **6** *yet for us there is but one God, the Father, from whom are all things and we exist for Him; and one Lord, Jesus Christ, by whom are all things, and we exist through Him.*

Paul continued to discuss the existence of idols. He classified them as so-called gods. Thus he distinguished them from the true God. These false gods were not genuine; they were counterfeit gods. Nonetheless, they existed in their minds. This admission does not contradict the statement that "there is no such thing as an idol in the world" (v. 4). Rather, acknowledging the existence of false gods only qualified Paul's previous statement. The confession of one true God does not nullify the fact that people worship **many gods and many lords.** Denial of their deity and refusal to acknowledge their existence, however, are two distinct proposals. **In heaven and on earth** discloses the sphere in which these imitation divinities supposedly act as gods. In various religions the sun, the moon, and the stars all are worshiped as gods. Countless parts of creation, from rivers and mountains to trees and animals, are deemed to be divine. From these natural forces men and women create gods to bow dow to and worship.

Yet (v. 6) is emphatic. The word translates the strongest adversative conjunction in the Greek language. A vital difference endures between the one God and the pagan idols. Idols are fabricated by people. Thus, idols are the product of human beings who are created by the one, true God. God is the Creator. Nothing exists apart from His creative activity. In verse 6 Paul stated that Jesus is God's agent in creation and that people are created for God. Salvation is the completion of God's creative design. Christians exist in Christ to please the Father and Son. Nothing else is as consequential!

3. Influence Superior to Freedom (8:7-13)

The Corinthians were correct in their assessment that some Christians have more knowledge than others. They failed to realize, however, that these others were looking to Christians with more knowledge for direction.

Verse 7: *However not all men have this knowledge; but some, being accustomed to the idol until now, eat food as if it were sacrificed to an idol; and their conscience being weak is defiled.*

Those who worshiped idols regarded them as authentic gods and worthy of worship. These people did not have the knowledge that there is only one God. Even within the church at Corinth, however, some did not have sufficient faith to completely forget their previous life. They had been pagans far longer than they had been Christians.

In sacrificial systems eating meat sacrificed to a god denoted fellowship with that god. Thus, eating meat dedicated to another deity presented a dilemma to the mind of these weak Christians. They realized that there was only one God, but they could not escape past convictions. They considered participation in such meals to somehow authenticate these false gods. Even if the meat was purchased in the market or eaten in the home of a friend, the implication remained. Therefore, in the minds of these less knowledgeable Christians, eating the meat was sin.

The **conscience** refers to a person's faculty for making responsible moral judgment.[2] When the conscience is **defiled,** it no longer has the capability to determine what is proper. Incorrect discernment may give the weaker Christian false permission to do wrong.

Verse 8: *But food will not commend us to God; we are neither the worse if we do not eat, nor the better if we do eat.*

Eating a certain kind of food **will not commend us to God.** Dietary laws had their place in the Old Testament Era. Particular foods were classified as edible. Others were unclean and forbidden to be eaten.

Ceremonial holiness and good physical health were the result of compliance with these laws. However, diet alone cannot modify a person's character. Eating veal, for instance, does not make one a morally better person. Nor does eating pork make one evil. A person is neither better nor worse for having eaten a particular food. Nor is a person drawn closer to God by the variety of foods ingested. Dietary considerations have no impact on a person's spiritual health. After the resurrection of Christ, God's people realized these truths. Food regulations no longer had relevance. So Christians were free to eat whatever they desire (Acts 10:9-16).

Verse 9: *But take care that this liberty of yours does not somehow become a stumbling block to the weak.*

Paul had addressed his readers from the perspective of knowledge. Here he turned to a position of the believer's relationship with weaker Christians. Actions that have no moral value may acquire moral or immoral merit because the actions are done in the presence of others.

Paul changed from "we" (v. 8) to "you." He moved from universal truths that included him to a specific application, the situation in Corinth. The specific situation did not include him because he was located in Ephesus, not Corinth. The foods on his table had no influence on people hundreds of miles distant.

Christ had set the Corinthians free by His grace. As a result of Christ's death and resurrection, the Corinthians could eat any food they preferred. God gave them liberty, but the addition of the words *of yours* clearly illustrate that their understanding of this liberty was distorted. The Corinthians emphasized the privilege of liberty but neglected their personal responsibility toward others. They exercised their rights, but they did not give serious consideration to how the exercise of those rights might harm other people. And the believers did not have the right to harm other people. Their knowledge gave the believers confidence, but such confidence exerted an influence over those who were less assured.

The Corinthians' witness was a potential **stumbling block to the weak.** A stumbling block is anything that causes a Christian to stray from God's will. **Weak** points to the truth that every believer is at a different level of maturity. Jesus compared salvation to birth (John 3:3). His analogy was followed by various New Testament writers (1 Cor. 3:1-2; Heb. 5:12-14; 1 Pet. 2:1-2). Just as people begin physical life as helpless infants, new converts are dependent too. And their development and maturity are dependent on various factors. Spiritual development depends, for instance, on the frequency of Bible study as well as an understanding of how to apply what is learned. Sadly, many who have been Christians for years are still children in the faith.

Paul warned the Corinthians that eating meat sacrificed to idols might cause some believers to deviate from God's will. **Somehow** shows that there may be numerous ways this can occur. However, the end result was that the weaker believer committed sin. Paul's warning **but take care** presupposed serious consequences in the event these weaker Christians did stumble. Those with greater knowledge must be careful not to use their knowledge as an excuse to do something that would cause a fellow Christian to stumble.

Verse 10: *For if someone sees you, who have knowledge, dining in an idol's temple, will not his conscience, if he is weak, be strengthened to eat things sacrificed to idols?*

In the verses that follow, the attitude of the Corinthians is contrasted with that of Christ. The Corinthians selfishly insisted they could eat meat sacrificed to idols because those idols represented gods that did not really exist. Paul acknowledged that because these false gods were fictitious, the Corinthians did not worship them by eating meat sacrificed to them. However, the apostle insisted that another factor should be considered—the effect of their actions on other Christians. While the act of eating such meat was not bad, the harm it did to less mature Christians was wrong. Therefore, if eating meat that had been sacrificed to an idol would lead immature believers to sin, the Corinthians should not do it!

In 1 Corinthians 10:20-22 Paul would develop another consideration concerning pagan gods. While the false gods were nonentities, a very real and wicked power gave them potency. Demonic presence and power animated these false gods. So eating meat sacrificed to idols could be tantamount to satanic worship!

Paul asked a rhetorical question based on the most glaring case. Suppose a mature Christian received an invitation to a social event in one of the pagan temples. Realizing that the particular deity did not exist, the believer thought that attendance at the temple would do no spiritual harm. Therefore, the invitation was accepted. What happened when a less mature Christian witnessed the believer leaving the temple? Would not the weaker Christian also be encouraged likewise to partake of meat sacrificed to idols? Paul not only implied that the answer was yes; but insinuated that the effect on the weaker believer would be bad, not good. The weaker Christian inevitably would commit additional sins.

Verse 11: *For through your knowledge he who is weak is ruined, the brother for whose sake Christ died.*

Because of their **knowledge,** some of the Corinthians ate meat sacrificed to idols. Paul's words expressed sarcasm of those who had boasted that idols were nothing. The idols might lack power, but the Christian's action had force. Unfortunately, some less-mature converts had witnessed the misguided use of Christian freedom and were **ru-**

ined. This word did not mean they lost their salvation. But either from disillusionment with other Christians or naivete about an action, these weaker believers sinned. They then experienced the grave consequence of their error.

In contrast to the arrogance of the Corinthians, Christ demonstrated the ultimate consideration for those weaker than Himself. As the Creator and Ruler of all things, He possessed an inherent right to utilize creation as He pleased. He would have been within His prerogative to condemn and destroy any individual who sinned. However, Christ freely limited His divine privilege and authority. In His incarnation He identified Himself with humankind. He offered Himself as the sacrifice for our sins. Therefore, the person hurt by the haughty action of the Corinthians was also the individual for whom Christ died! He was identified as a brother, a genuine believer. Paul urged the Corinthian Christians to stop such action.

Verse 12: *And so, by sinning against the brethren and wounding their conscience when it is weak, you sin against Christ.*

The original meaning of the verb **sin** was "to miss the mark." The sense "to commit an offense against someone" was a derived meaning.[3] Causing another Christian to sin certainly misses the mark of what that person has a right to expect from another believer. Causing another Christian to stumble violates the Christian relationship. Causing another to stumble impedes the spiritual growth of less mature believers.

The weaker **brethren** were part of the body of Christ. Any sin against them was a transgression against Christ. Therefore, Corinthians were hurting themselves, the weaker brother, and the cause of Christ!

Verse 13: *Therefore, if food causes my brother to stumble, I will never eat meat again, so that I will not cause my brother to stumble.*

The spiritual welfare of a brother is to take precedence over personal freedom. Love is more important than knowledge or liberty. More mature Christians always put the interest of weaker Christians ahead of their own. Preferring others is the natural consequence of Christian love. Preferring others is the attitude of a heart that is right with God. When we are right with God, we act as God would act.

A Christian should not use this verse to coerce another believer into a desired behavior. The repetition of the first personal pronouns **I** and **my** points to Paul's personal decision in this specific case. At other times, however, right actions may not be as clearly defined. There are some issues about which Christians have agreed to disagree. For instance, differences concerning the millennium should not affect the fellowship between Christians. On the other hand, certain differences should affect relationships. If an individual denies the deity of Jesus or

His resurrection, fellowship might signify acceptance of heretical theology. There are numerous areas where the effects of differences require serious and prayerful consideration. But we always must love those who are at another level of spiritual maturity. Our love for each other is our Christian validation to the unsaved people of the world (John 13:35).

For Further Study

1. Read about sacrifice in the *Holman Bible Dictionary,* pages 1218-1220, or in another Bible dictionary.

2. Read about knowledge in the *Holman Bible Dictionary,* pages 852-853, or in another Bible dictionary.

3. Read "First-Century Temples" in the Winter 1991 issue of the *Biblical Illustrator.*

4. What are some differences that should not affect fellowship between Christians? What are some differences that rightly have implications for fellowship?

5. What are some practices in your church among long-time Christians that might negatively impact new Christians' relationship with Christ?

---

1 "Tiny bugs hook illegal fish ring," *The Columbus, Georgia, Ledger-Enquirer* (Thursday, February 23, 1995), sec. a, 2.

2 Raymond Bryan Brown, "1 Corinthians," *Broadman Bible Commentary,* vol. 10, p. 339.

3 *New International Dictionary of New Testament Theology,* 1976 ed., "Sin" by Walther Günther, 3:577.

June 29, 1997

Taking Care of Our Leaders

Background Passage: 1 Corinthians 9:1-18
Focal Passage: 1 Corinthians 9:1-14

Introduction

I finished my first service as pastor of my very first church. My emotions had never been higher. Everything had gone better than expected. When two deacons called me aside, I anticipated their praise. Instead, they said, "Preacher, would you be upset if we cut your salary?"

What could I say? I wanted to leave and never come back. But I was certain God had placed me in that church. Therefore, resignation was never a viable consideration. Nonetheless, doubts about coming to that congregation and thoughts concerning my ability to trust promises they made began to creep into my mind.

I managed to respond to the deacon's question by saying that my acceptance of the church's call was not based on money. I knew my somewhat-forced reply was true. Yet contemplation of an inability to provide for my family caused me to wonder about the future.

The deacon continued, "We know what we committed to pay you. But preacher, in the history of our church we never have received that much money in tithes and offerings. We just aren't sure we can pay that amount."

The amount of money in question was not large, but I knew the deacon's words were true. All I could do was trust to God. That night the deacons met with me prior to the evening service. I listened as the chairman spoke. "We met this afternoon to pray about cutting your salary. And we all agreed that our church made a commitment to you and your family. We plan to honor our word. We will trust God to provide the offerings required to meet this commitment." I remained the pastor of that small, rural congregation for six years. It was one of the most wonderful periods of my ministry. God blessed us, and the church grew dramatically. And not once did the church fail to honor its responsibility to care for its pastor.

1 Corinthians 9:1-18
   1. Paul's Assertion of His Apostleship (9:1-2)
   2. Paul's Rights as an Apostle (9:3-6)
   3. The Principle of Material Support for Spiritual Leaders (9:7-14)

4. Paul's Refusal of His Rights and Benefits (9:15-18)

The Background

Paul's enemies apparently had maligned his apostleship and his authority. Their attack included questions about his personal conduct as it related to the office of apostle. They pointed out differences between Paul's behavior and that of other apostles. For example, Paul's marital status differed from other church leaders. Most were married, but he was single. Furthermore, those who disliked Paul raised the issue of his earning income as a tentmaker. Many other ministers did not work a secular job but derived an income from their ministry. Thus many Corinthians concluded that Paul must not be a genuine apostle. Others believed that Paul was obligated to preach without compensation. They argued that if he received material support he was guilty of preaching as a means to obtain wealth! How could Paul correct these erroneous opinions without completely alienating one group or affirming the fallacy of another? These charges seemed to put Paul in a no-win situation.

The Lesson Passage

1. Paul's Assertion of His Apostleship (9:1-2)

The questions Paul asked in these verses were typical of a popular first-century teaching method. The grammar in the original Greek indicates that an affirmative answer was expected to the question. Thus Paul phrased the questions so that he and his readers might find a consensus of opinion regarding certain matters pertaining to the issue of apostleship.

Verse 1: *Am I not free? Am I not an apostle? Have I not seen Jesus our Lord? Are you not my work in the Lord?*

Paul turned from his discussion of Christian freedom to its application in his own life. He asked if he was not **free.** A negative response would deny his salvation experience. His transformation from church persecutor to church missionary and builder made such a conclusion indefensible. An affirmative answer asserted that like every believer, Christ had set Paul free. Therefore, he was free to make his own choices. By asking this question the apostle established that his refusal to accept pay at Corinth was a personal decision, not an obligation to the Corinthian church.

Next, Paul raised the issue of his apostleship. The term **apostle** denoted a person sent to accomplish a specific mission. The apostle had the authority of the person who sent him. In the New Testament the term occurs in a wide sense and a narrow sense. The wider sense identified an apostle as a commissioned representative of the church (Rom. 16:7; 2 Cor. 8:23; Phil. 2:25). However, the narrow sense is the most common usage. The title designates a specific group of church leaders. The office was limited to those who were witnesses of the resurrected Christ and who proclaimed the gospel message.[1]

The twelve apostles primarily refer to those men Jesus chose as disciples. After Judas Iscariot's treachery, the early church selected Matthias as his replacement. If Paul did not profess inclusion in this group, he surely claimed equality with them because he felt that he met the requirements of an apostle. However, the content of his protest here suggests he believed he rightly belonged with the twelve.

Paul had encountered the risen Lord on the road to Damascus (Acts 9:3-8). He argued that this encounter was Christ's last appearance after His resurrection (1 Cor. 15:8). Therefore, the incident qualified Paul to be included among those who were apostles.

The church at Corinth was established and grew as the result of Paul's preaching ministry. Thus, those who disputed his apostleship must confute his successful labor as an apostle. The record of that success was self-evident.

Verse 2: *If to others I am not an apostle, at least I am to you; for you are the seal of my apostleship in the Lord.*

The Corinthian church authenticated Paul's apostleship. The implication of Paul's assertion was clear. If he was an apostle in the geographical territory around Corinth, he was an apostle everywhere. The criticism of his enemies did not alter this fact.

A *seal* was a signet inscribed with a distinctive mark to identify its owner. The mark was placed on documents or objects by pressing the seal into soft clay or wax. The seal had legal importance in the first century. It indicated ownership, thereby protecting property from theft. On documents a seal served as a signature authorizing the written content of the manuscript. In the New Testament the term has a figurative sense of confirming or authenticating something.[2] By referring to the Corinthians as the seal of his apostleship, Paul asserted that his office could not be stolen from him by the false testimony of his enemies. The church in Corinth was a divine signature on Paul's commission to the apostolic office.

Paul's words encourage us to affirm publicly those individuals who have ministered faithfully to us and with us. Our expressions can serve as evidence that these individuals are genuine ministers of the gospel. In an era when debased ministers receive so much publicity, most pastors and staff members are serving faithfully and they appreciate recognition of their faithful service. Such expressions of thanksgiving and recognition are an encouragement to faithful ministers.

2. Paul's Rights as an Apostle (9:3-6)

Paul set forth the rights of an apostle. His presentation was framed as a legal defense of his own position. His usage of first person plural pronouns attest his inclusion among those who enjoyed the rights of an apostle. In verses 5-6 Paul illustrated his rights with three examples.

Verses 3-4: *My defense to those who examine me is this: 4 Do we not have a right to eat and drink?*

Examine denotes a judicial investigation. Paul's opponents had attacked him viciously, so he countered with a judicial rebuttal. The question expects a yes answer. Paul's question in this verse may refer to his eating meat sacrificed to idols (1 Cor. 8:1-13). If so, the apostle defended his right to eat meat of his own choice. Paul's critics did not possess the right to dictate what he could or could not eat. Paul's choice of foods was his personal right. Today, every local congregation needs to respect its minister's privacy and privileges.

Another interpretation of Paul's question is that it implied the right of the apostle to be supported by the local congregation. The church should free its ministers from anxiety about material matters so that they may engage fully in God's service. Such support makes their ministry possible.[3]

Both interpretations possess certain merits. Perhaps Paul's words convey both ideas. God's calling to ministry meant that God's servant had a right to certain personal privileges. Serving God meant that he could expect support from churches. The two ideas seem to be two sides of the same coin.

Verse 5: *Do we not have a right to take along a believing wife, even as the rest of the apostles and the brothers of the Lord and Cephas?*

Ministers of the gospel enjoy the privilege of marriage. The early church fathers interpreted *a believing wife* as a reference to female missionary assistants. Most certainly, however, the reference is to a wife.[4] Thus the reference is to a spouse who is a Christian. The pastor, staff, and other leaders of a church have the right to a family life. Consideration of their private time allows them to enjoy both a private and family life.

Apparently, during the first century most ministers traveled with their wives. Paul singled out three examples from his contemporaries as precedents to establish his own right to do likewise. The phrase *the rest of the apostles* seems to refer to the original twelve disciples.

James, Joses, Judas, and Simon (Mark 6:3) were the sons of Mary and Joseph. Hence, they were *the brothers of the Lord.* The four were all born after Jesus. They apparently did not follow their elder Brother until after His resurrection. James became the leader of the church in

Jerusalem and the author of the New Testament epistle which bears his name. Judas (Jude) wrote the New Testament letter of Jude (Jude 1). The prestige of these men, especially James, was widespread.

Cephas was Simon Peter's Aramaic name. His marriage is attested in the Gospels (Matt. 8:14; Mark 1:30; Luke 4:38). The specific reference to Peter may indicate that he and his wife previously had visited Corinth. Paul may have mentioned Peter's name to influence the party that followed Peter, or he may have named Peter merely because of his fame. Peter did more than anyone to prevent early Christianity from fragmenting into distinct groups. He served as a bridge between Gentile and Jewish communities.

Verse 6: *Or do only Barnabas and I not have a right to refrain from working?*

Paul continued to point to his rights as an apostle. His next question presumed a negative answer! ***Barnabas*** was a prominent leader in the early church. He became Paul's partner on his first missionary journey. Prior to the second missionary journey, the two men separated after a dispute about taking John Mark on the second trip (Acts 15:36-40). Thereafter, Silas became Paul's companion, and John Mark traveled with Barnabas. Silas was with Paul during his ministry in Corinth. Why Paul mentioned Barnabas in verse 6 is not known unless Silas was with Paul during his ministry in Corinth. Apparently, Barnabas supported himself like Paul did through some secular occupation.

Some people at Corinth observed Paul's habit of supporting himself by tent-making. They compared Paul's working with the tangible support given those who were recognized as apostles. Therefore, they concluded Paul was not on par with these other apostles. Others apparently grumbled when Paul ceased to support himself! Later, Paul would admit that his secular employment had been inadequate. He survived only because other churches had supplied his personal needs (2 Cor. 11:8-9; Phil 4:15-16).

3. The Principle of Material Support for Spiritual Leaders (9:7-14)

Paul proceeded to demonstrate that ministers (including himself) deserved material support. First, he appealed to daily life and the ordinary laws of human fairness. He used an analogy of three common workers to support his position for ministerial sustenance. Then he appealed to the Old Testament. He drew both a temporal illustration and a religious example from the Scripture.

Verse 7: *Who at any time serves as a soldier at his own expense? Who plants a vineyard and does not eat the fruit of it? Or who tends a flock and does not use the milk of the flock?*

Paul asked three questions about benefits of certain vocations. All three expect the reader to answer, "Nobody."

Soldier, farmer, and shepherd were familiar occupations in the first century. Roman soldiers were paid 250 denarii a year for military service. The government deducted the cost of equipment, clothing, and rations from these wages. But the pay was still sufficient to more than cover all expenses. Bonuses gave the soldiers hope that the military would be a lucrative career.[5] But life in the army was arduous and dangerous. No one would serve without some compensation.

Vineyards were prominent in the ancient agriculture. However, they required continual and intensive attention. Anyone planting a vineyard expected to enjoy its fruit.

Milk was a staple of the Jewish diet. Vendors sold it in the street markets of every city. Although cows provided some milk, sheep and goats were the most common source of milk. Shepherds took milk for their use from their flock.

The point of these analogies was to point out to the Corinthians that Paul had the right to expect pay for his spiritual labor just as the soldier, farmer, and shepherd did for their physical labor.

Verse 8: *I am not speaking these things according to human judgment, am I? Or does not the Law also say these things?*

The grammatical construction of this question indicates that a negative answer is expected. Paul had established that the ordinary rules of human conduct dictated that ministers should receive material support. In this verse he proceeded to demonstrate that the principle did not rest solely on **human judgment.** He used another rhetorical question to remind his readers that the same principle occurs in Scripture. The term **Law** generally refers to the first five books of the Old Testament. However, on occasion it may denote the whole of Old Testament Scripture. Here, either sense would be appropriate. Paul's point about receiving support from those he served was not based on human deduction, but divine revelation.

Verse 9: *For it is written in the Law of Moses, "You shall not muzzle the ox while he is threshing." God is not concerned about oxen, is He?*

Paul quoted Deuteronomy 25:4. The Old Testament passage demonstrated that even the lowest creatures were provided for by God. After being harvested sheaves of grain were spread on a threshing floor of earth or stone. Animals, usually cattle, trampled the sheaves to separate the grain from the husks. The husks were removed by winnowing. This process involved tossing the mixed chaff and grain into the air. The wind then blew the useless chaff away, but the grain fell back onto the floor. The law prohibited Israelite farmers from binding the mouth of the animals used in threshing. These creatures were permitted to eat some of the grain as they worked.

Paul's question does not mean that God is indifferent to the needs of animals. God's provisions reflect divine regard for their needs (Gen. 1:30; Matt. 6:26). However, the quotation from Deuteronomy falls between two passages concerning human relationships. Therefore, the law regarding not muzzling a working animal always may have been figurative. Regardless of its original intent, Paul's application stressed that God is more concerned with people than animals.

Verse 10: *Or is He speaking altogether for our sake? Yes, for our sake it was written, because the plowman ought to plow in hope, and the thresher to thresh in hope of sharing the crops.*

Paul asked what was the primary application of Deuteronomy 25:4. There may have been a literal meaning, but was it secondary to the spiritual sense? Paul answered his own question. *Yes,* the ancient farming law applied to the believers.

A *plowman* and a *thresher* have different skills. Their separate tasks are performed at different seasons of the year. The analogy signifies that the work of Christian ministers varies. All deserve support.

Verse 11: *If we sowed spiritual things in you, is it too much if we reap material things from you?*

Paul continued the analogy of agriculture, but the application of his argument became specific in this verse. The grammatical construction of the conditional sentence indicates that the condition had been fulfilled. Paul had planted a crop in the city of Corinth and deserved to reap from its harvest. His seeds were *spiritual,* the gospel he proclaimed. The seeds had sprouted and grown into a church. Paul deserved to gather *material* fruit from this crop.

Verse 12: *If others share the right over you, do we not more? Nevertheless, we did not use this right, but we endure all things so that we will cause no hindrance to the gospel of Christ.*

The *others* cannot be identified. Perhaps Paul pointed to Apollos (Acts 19:1). Possibly, Peter received gifts from this congregation.

People criticized the traveling Greek philosophers for accepting a fee when they spoke. Some believed their lectures would be influenced more by the fee than the truth. Like the philosophers, the minister who is paid for his services risks preaching to accommodate his listeners. The minister who receives no compensation has no accountability to those with whom he works.

Paul was the first person to proclaim the gospel in Corinth. He feared his audience might equate his message with some speech designed to earn a good income. The word *hindrance* only occurs here in the entire New Testament. It referred to the destruction of a road to prevent pursuit by an enemy.[6] Paul did not wish for anything to distract his audience when he preached. So Paul relinquished his right to material support in order to avoid charges of duplicity. As stated above,

Paul's decision to preach without compensation while in Corinth was possible because other churches supported him financially.

Verse 13: *Do you not know that those who perform sacred services eat the food of the temple, and those who attend regularly to the altar have their share from the altar?*

Next, Paul illustrated his proposition by the example of the Jewish priesthood. Priests were supported from the various offerings commanded by God. The Levites were given the tithe, not land, as an inheritance in Canaan.

Verse 14: *So also the Lord directed those who proclaim the gospel to get their living from the gospel.*

Paul applied the Old Testament principle of support for the priesthood to New Testament ministers. He apparently was familiar with Christ's statement, "for the worker is worthy of his support" (Matt. 10:10). Paul also quoted the statement in his letter to Timothy (1 Tim. 5:18).

4. Paul's Refusal of His Rights and Benefits (9:15-18)

Paul appealed to his own abandonment of a right that was his in order to encourage the readers, if the necessity should arise, to abandon their own rights concerning Christian liberty. Paul was not complaining that the Corinthians did not support him. He insisted, "I gave up my rights while I was among you. And I did so freely." "To die" does not imply Paul might starve if the Corinthians failed to support him. Rather, he preferred to die rather than lose his independence.

Paul was trying to remove all appearance of haughtiness from his tone. There was no merit to him in his preaching of the gospel of Jesus Christ. Paul preached the message about Christ out of a moral compulsion from his divine calling. Had he gone against his divine commission, Paul would have been miserable. And he would have invited divine judgment against himself.

Paul insisted, "My reward is that I can preach without charge." The motivation for ministry should not be financial gain. The true minister preaches because of a divine calling. Nonetheless, the church has a stewardship to support its pastor and staff.

For Further Study

1. How can adults affirm publicly those who have ministered to them?

2. Read "The Apostolic Office" in the Fall 1991 issue of the *Biblical Illustrator.*

3. Read "Paul's Means of Support in Ministry" in the Fall 1994 issue of the *Biblical Illustrator.*

4. Evaluate the material provision for the pastor and the other paid staff members of your own church. Does it meet their needs?

1 *Holman Bible Dictionary,* 1991 ed., "Disciples; Apostles" by Robert Sloan, 362-64.

2 *Dictionary of New Testament Theology,* 1978 ed., "Seal" by Reinier Schippers, 3:497-99

3 C. W. Brister, "The Ministry in I Corinthians," *Southwestern Journal of Theology* 26 (Fall 1988): 30.

4 *Dictionary of New Testament Theology,* 1978 ed., "Woman" by Herwart Vorlander and Colin Brown, 3;1055; Albrecht Oepek, "γυνή," *Theological Dictionary of the New Testament,* (Grand Rapids: Wm. B. Eerdmans Pub. Co., 1964), 1:776.

5 Michael Grant, *The Army of the Caesars* (New York: Charles Scribner's Sons, 1974), xxxii-xxxiii, 14-15.

6 Brown, "1 Corinthians," *Broadman Bible Commentary,* vol 10, 42.

July 6, 1997

Winning as Many as Possible

Background Passage: 1 Corinthians 9:19–11:1
Focal Passages: 1 Corinthians 9:19-23; 10:23-24,31-11:1

Introduction

Charlotte Diggs Moon grew up among the landed gentry of antebellum Virginia. In 1873 Lottie, as she was known to her friends, was appointed by the International Mission Board of the Southern Baptist Convention as a missionary to China. When she first arrived in China, she opened a school for girls as a method for missions. But she continued to dress and behave as an American. Everywhere she went she encountered hatred and ridicule from the Chinese. The native population considered her an unwanted foreigner. She constantly was the target for a verbal barrage of "devil woman."

Despite the barrier of prejudice, Lottie Moon loved the Chinese people. She developed a strong desire for direct personal evangelism and traveled throughout North China preaching the gospel to women. Then she moved to Pingtu in order to establish a work in that city. Lottie decided to change her methodology once more. The harsh winters in the region forced her to adopt the padded robe worn by the Chinese women. The new apparel made a dramatic difference in her relations with the Chinese people. No longer did Lottie receive the scorn of those she met on the streets. Her new strategy worked.

Lottie became a friend and neighbor to those in her community. She explained her approach to missions by the statement "Demonstrate a Chinese-style Christian life," which means, "We must go out and live among them, manifesting the gentle, loving spirit of our Lord. We need to make friends before we can hope to make converts."[1] To Southern Baptists, the name of Lottie Moon is synonymous with missions. Her advice still works. Christians are able to win more people to Christ by being sensitive to the backgrounds, needs, and circumstances of individual unbelievers.

1 Corinthians 9:19–11:1
1. Serving Others That They Might Be Saved (9:19-27)
2. An Example from Israel's History (10:1-22)
3. Seeking the Good of Others That They Might Be Saved (10:23–11:1)

The Background

Certainly, some Corinthians asked, "Why should we yield to a weaker person?" Evangelism was Paul's answer. He applied to evangelism the same ideas set forth in his previous discussion on eating meat sacrificed to idols (1 Cor. 8:1-13). Paul illustrated these principles in his own life. He put the salvation of others above his own comfort and interest. Paul recalled lessons the Hebrew people learned during their earliest years of existence to bolster his argument. During the time of the exodus and wilderness wandering, the people had moments of great spiritual experience and loyalty to God. However, they also committed sins of self-indulgence and rebellion against God's leadership. Those times of rebellion cost them dearly in loss of life and loss of opportunity. Paul warned the Corinthian Christians not to abuse their new freedom in Christ for self-indulgence. Rather, they were to use that freedom to win others to faith in Christ.

The Lesson Passage

1. Serving Others That They Might Be Saved (9:19-27)

Paul's life revealed that he was willing to abandon his own rights to win others for Christ. A series of comparisons communicated this attitude. First, Paul described the abandonment of his rights in political terminology (9:19). Then, he used a religious analogy (9:20-23). And finally, Paul illustrated his zeal by an athletic metaphor (9:24-27).

Verse 19: *For though I am free from all men, I have made myself a slave to all, so that I may win more.*

Christ set His disciples free. Therefore, we are truly free (John 8:36). *The New International Version of the New Testament* expresses the sense of *I am free from all men* well. It reads, "I am free and belong to no man." No human being has dominion over a Christian.

In first-century secular society the term *free* had a political sense. A person who belonged to the state was a free citizen as contrasted with a slave or a foreigner. That person could participate in public debates concerning civic matters. A free person operated within the sovereignty and law of his or her state.[2] A free Roman citizen was the foremost status of society. Paul was proud of his own Roman citizenship. He was not ashamed to admit His citizenship was his by birth, but he gladly would surrender it for the sake of the gospel. Not only would he surrender his citizenship, Paul willfully would enter the lowest political level— slavery!

Paul frequently used the noun *slave* to emphasize his absolute submission to Christ. A slave was devoid of all personal rights. The slave's sole purpose for existence was to carry out the wishes of the master. But in this verse *all* people, not Christ, were Paul's master. Paul did not mean that he permitted all people to control his life. Rather, he strived to serve all people in order that he might introduce those he served to salvation.

Attitudes toward slavery were vastly different in the first century. Modern disgust over the ownership of one human being by another simply was not a factor. Slavery was merely another social, or class, distinction. Slavery was universally accepted in the Roman Empire as indispensable to civilized society. Slaves constituted a major element of the workforce. They included professional people such as physicians, teachers, and administrators. They also included domestic servants and manual laborers, and even gladiators. People could not imagine how commerce and public life could survive without slaves.[3] They were a significant element within every major city. The slave population of Rome was between 200,000 and 250,000, over one quarter of the city's total inhabitants.[4]

Paul's approach to evangelism was based on making deliberate choices. These choices adapted his behavior to those to whom he was witnessing. One of the guidelines Paul used in determining his personal conduct was its impact on others. He asked, "How many people will my behavior influence?" Paul chose the behavior that permitted him to witness effectively to the largest number of people.

Verse 20: *To the Jews I became as a Jew, so that I might win Jews; to those who are under the Law, as under the Law though not being myself under the Law, so that I might win those who are under the Law;*

In witnessing to the Jews, Paul sought to identify with them. He emphasized that Jesus was the Messiah (Acts 13:23; 17:3; 18:5,28). Unless harm was done to Christian truth, Paul often conformed to Jewish custom (Acts 16:3; 18:18; 21:26). On these occasions the apostle believed there was opportunity to advance the cause of Christ by relating to the Jews as a Jew.

Always Paul weighed his decisions. He refused to compromise the gospel for the sake of pleasing people. Adaptation involves cultivation of common experiences, but it should never allow any alteration of the truth. An example of Paul's stand for the truth occurred at Antioch. There Paul publicly rebuked Peter when Peter's efforts to appease the Jews distorted the truth of the gospel (Gal. 2:11-21).

Those who are under the Law do not form a separate group from the Jews. The phrase emphasized the Mosaic legal code. Paul no longer lived by the Law as a means of securing his salvation. Rather, he lived by faith in Christ. However, in order to **win those who are under the Law,** Paul showed sensitivity to the Jewish interpretation of religion and subjected himself to the law for their sake.

Gentiles considered Jewish customs strange and irrational. No better proof of Paul's accommodating spirit could be given to his Gentile readers than by pointing out that he subjected himself to the difficult and meticulous Jewish laws in order to witness to the Jews.

Verse 21: *to those who are without law, as without law, though not being without the law of God but under the law of Christ, so that I might win those who are without law.*

The Gentiles are **those who are without law.** Paul lived as a Gentile. This did not imply that he became a lawless or immoral person. Rather, Paul tried to empathize with the Gentile perspective of life and salvation. He did not conform his meals to Jewish dietary laws but ate the fare of those to whom he was ministering. Nor did Paul restrict his contacts to prevent ritual defilement. He ministered to everyone, Jew and Gentile alike.

Not without the law of God is a reference to Paul, not to Gentiles. Paul did not mean that he lived a lawless, sinful life as he sought to identify with unsaved Gentiles. Rather, he referred to his being subject to Christ and His law, not the written code of the Old Testament. Being without the law of God and being under the law of Christ is not a license to sin. On the other hand, submission to Christ is a submission to holiness. So, make no mistake, when Paul identified with lawless Gentiles his life was subject to Christ.

The **law of Christ** refers to the centrality of love. During the last supper Jesus commanded His disciples to love one another (John15:12). He revealed that love for one another would be the distinguishing characteristic of His followers (John 13:35).

Verse 22: *To the weak I became weak, that I might win the weak; I have become all things to all men, so that I may by all means save some.*

Weak refers to immature Christians, both Jew and Gentile. Paul empathized with the immature and was considerate of them. He nurtured them toward a maturing faith. Helping new converts mature was important missionary work to Paul. Too often, contemporary Christianity neglects the ministry of spiritual nurture.

Paul was compassionate, sympathetic, and willing to relinquish his own rights in matters of no moral significance in order to gain another convert for Christ or to strengthen a weaker Christian. **That I may by all means save some** must be understood in light of all other Scripture. Salvation is an act of divine grace. It is the result of Christ's death and resurrection. Paul knew that he could never save a sinner. Only God can save an individual, but He works through His people.[5]

Verse 23: *I do all things for the sake of the gospel, so that I may become a fellow partaker of it.*

Paul was not guilty of expediency. He never compromised his fundamental doctrines, nor did he surrender the commitment to his mission. Paul always kept in mind the question "Will my behavior enhance sharing the gospel?" Everything Paul did was done for a single purpose—the expansion of the Christian faith. He did those things that caused others to listen to the message about Christ.

Paul did not receive monetary reward for his preaching. Rather, he fulfilled his calling as an apostle and shared in the benefits of the gospel. While the phrase *fellow partaker* reflects an awareness of Paul's own needs, it stressed his sharing with others. The apostle desired to share in the blessings of the gospel.

In verses 24-27 Paul switched to an athletic metaphor to encourage the Corinthians to follow his example of witnessing. The Isthmian games were held every two years. In a track and field race, winning was the competitor's goal. Only one person could finish in first place. Therefore, everything the runner did was calculated to win the race. The winner received a wreath of pine, but he wore it proudly because it signified he was a winner in the games.

Participants had to sign an oath that they had trained for 10 months. If men sacrificed for such a fading, poor crown, should not the believer sacrifice for the cause of witnessing about Christ to a lost world?

The runner and the boxer each had a purpose in their practice. They sought to perfect their skills in order to win the athletic contest against the opponent. They subdued their bodies so that after proclaiming to others the rules of the contest they would not break the rules and be eliminated from competition. To be ejected from the games was a deadly insult in ancient Greece.

The figures of the runner and boxer described Paul's single-minded pursuit of evangelism. He disciplined his whole person for the task. Paul's mention of disqualification did not suggest the loss of salvation but the loss of effective witness because of an undisciplined life. Such commitment is needed by all of us as well if we are to be effective servants for Christ.

2. An Example from Israel's History (10:1-22)

What is the connection of chapter 10 with chapters 8—9? How does chapter 10 fit into Paul's discussion of eating meat sacrificed to idols?

In chapter 8 Paul taught the principle that the believers were free to do whatever the Scriptures do not forbid. If the Corinthians loved others as God would have them love others, Paul said that they should limit their liberty for the sake of weaker believers.

In chapter 9 Paul illustrated from his own life and ministry his point about limiting personal liberty. He said that in order to keep the

Corinthians from thinking he was preaching for money, he accepted no wages for preaching. However, Paul had the right to accept wages. The Old Testament taught the same truth—workers can expect pay for labor. Paul also pointed out how he modified his lifestyle to witness more effectively. His behavioral change, though, was in harmony with the Lord's will.

In chapter 10 Paul showed how using one's freedom can affect one's own life. Many of the Corinthian believers thought they were strong enough spiritually to associate with pagans socially and religiously as long as they did not participate in idolatry or immorality.

Paul warned the Corinthians they were deceived. Abusing liberty harmed weak believers and put their own lives in danger. The mature believer should not jeopardize his or her liberty by playing around with temptation and sin. The problem with the Corinthians was that they were too confident. They had no fear they might fall from holiness and usefulness in service. So, Paul brought to their attention how ancient Israel had suffered from over-confident living. He mentioned their idolatry, immorality, and their complaining against God. Then in verses 14-22 Paul explained why idolatry is especially abominable to God. It might not be morally wrong to eat meat offered to an idol, but it is sin to practice idol worship. Although the Corinthians might attend pagan functions and think nothing of it, they were not free to participate in false worship.

Paul appealed to his readers to shun idol feasts. Attempting to get as close to idol worship as possible without becoming part of it is dangerous. A Christian does not have the privilege to see how close to the world he or she can live. Too much compromise exists already. Paul's reference to "wise men" (10:15) was not sarcasm but was an honest appeal, an emotional plea for right action by the Corinthians. He wanted them the conform to the right way, the way of love for the weaker brother and the way of holiness in relationship to a pagan world.

3. Seeking the Good of Others That They Might Be Saved (10:23–11:1)

Having forbidden the Corinthians from participation in idol feasts, Paul deliberated about the broader question of meat sacrificed to idols. Much of the meat sold in the public markets of Corinth was the leftovers from animals sacrificed in the city's temples. Clearly taking part in idolatrous worship was wrong. But did that imply that when a believer purchased meat in the market he or she must determine if the meat came from a local pagan temple?

Verse 23: *All things are lawful, but not all things are profitable.*

All things are lawful, but not all things edify.

The first sentence of this verse also occurs in 1 Corinthians 6:12. The statement **all things are lawful** originally may have been made by Paul with regard to Jewish dietary laws. It occurs twice here and twice in 1 Corinthians 6:12. The Corinthians seem to have used this maxim to justify their conduct. They believed that what was done by the physical body did not damage one's spiritual life. Paul accepted the basic truthfulness of the original slogan but qualified its operation.

Paul had shown by his own example that Christian liberty must be exercised in light of its influence on weaker Christians. The Christian life is not regulated by law codes. Christians must do more than determine if an action is allowed. Christians should also ask, "What are the consequences of those actions?" They should ask "Will this help my brother or sister in Christ?" The spiritual growth of other Christians is a vital consideration for determining right or wrong actions.

Verse 24: *Let no one seek his own good, but that of his neighbor.*

Christian liberty is not a license to do as one pleases. The welfare of others is more important than personal gratification.

Paul instructed his readers to buy meat in the market with a clear conscience. They should not ask religious questions about the source of the meat. He said for them not to worry about where the meat came from, just eat it. And they should give thanks to God for He is the Creator of life and all living creatures belong to Him.

Verse 31: *Whether, then, you eat or drink or whatever you do, do all to the glory of God.*

Here is another of Paul's guidelines for determining personal behavior. If an action is in a questionable action, the believer should ask, "Will my behavior glorify God?" All Christian activity should be done for **the glory of God.**

The noun **glory** describes that which makes a person or object impressive. **Glory** is that which distinguishes one individual from other people and earns the respect of the community.[6] When applied to God, the word suggests the manifestation of His power or the declaration of His will. So **glory** refers to the revelation of His presence. Therefore, Paul determined that all of his actions would always reveal the presence of God in his life to those around him.

Verse 32: *Give no offense either to Jews or to Greeks or to the church of God;*

Another question one should ask for determining behavior in uncertain circumstances is "Will my behavior offend anyone?" Christians should exhibit Christian concern for others. They need to make every effort to foster spiritual encouragement, not to cause spiritual defeat.

The inclusion of **the church of God** among those to whom believers were to *give no offense* insinuates that the **Jews** and the **Greeks** were non-Christians, Jewish non-believers, and Gentile pagans. Christians, therefore, should be as sensitive as possible to both non-Christian and Christians alike.

Verse 33: *just as I also please all men in all things, not seeking my own profit but the profit of the many, so that they may be saved.*

Paul was attentive to his relationship with other people because he was concerned about their salvation. The apostle was committed to self-restraint. He was not self-centered in his conduct. In everything he sought the benefit of the majority rather than his own self-interest.

In his evangelistic efforts Paul sought to establish some kind of personal connection. In the Jewish synagogues he began witnessing by speaking on some point of mutual agreement about God. For example, at Psidian Antioch Paul recited the history of God's provisions for Israel (Acts 13:16-22). With pagans, he discovered other approaches. For example, Paul comforted the Philippian jailer with the assurance that no prisoners had escaped (Acts 16:28).

11:1: *Be imitators of me, just as I also am of Christ.*

Paul's life was a visible reproduction of the life of the Lord Jesus Christ. Therefore, he called on the Corinthian Christians to imitate his life. Yet in doing so Paul directed their attention away from himself. The only justification for them to imitate him was that he imitated the Lord. Paul wanted them to duplicate those features of the life of Christ that they saw in his life. Paul's purpose in having them copy him was not to draw attention to himself. It was to reveal Christ to others.

Jesus lived a perfect life. Even when that perfection demanded His death on the cross, no defect was found. During his early adult years, Paul violently opposed the consequences of Christ's perfect life. Then Paul met the risen Christ in a dramatic confrontation on the Damascus Road. For the rest of his life, Paul desired and endeavored to become more like Jesus.

The Corinthians had never seen Jesus. Most had never heard of Him. They lived as if He never was born. Then one day Paul arrived in their city. In his life they could see a reflection of Jesus. Like Paul, some of them decided to trust in Jesus and become more like Him. For 2,000 years the blessings of salvation have continued. You and I are links in the chain. B. B. McKinney put the concept in a hymn. "While passing through this world of sin, And others your life shall view, Be clean and pure without, within, Let others see Jesus in you."[7]

For Further Study

1. Read "Paul's Use of Athletic Metaphors" in the Spring 1993 issue of the *Biblical Illustrator*.

2. Read about slavery in the *Holman Bible Dictionary,* pages 1286-1287, or in another Bible dictionary.

3. Paul adapted to the customs of those to whom he witnessed. Investigate the culture of someone different from yourself and discover new ways to relate to them and to share the gospel with them.

---

1 William R. Estep, *Whole Gospel, Whole World* (Nashville: Broadman & Holman, 1994), 146-48.

2 Heinrich Schlier, "ἐλεύθερος, ἐλευθερόω, ἐλευθερία, ἀπελεύθερος, *Theological Dictionary of the New Testament,* (Grand Rapids: Wm. B. Eerdmans Pub. Co., 1964), 2:487-88.

3 Eduard Lohse, *The New Testament Environment,* trans. John E. Steely (Nashville: Abingdon, 1976), 213.

4 J. P. V. D. Balsdon, *Romans and Aliens* (Chapel Hill, North Carolina: University of North Carolina Press, 1979), 12.

5 Walter T. Conner, *The Gospel of Redemption* (Nashville: Broadman Press, 1945), 297.

6 Walther Eichrodt, *Theology of the Old Testament,* trans. J. A. Baker, *Old Testament Library,* ed. G. Ernest Wright, John Bright, James Barr, and Peter Ackroyd (Philadelphia: Westminster Press, 1967), vol. 2, 30; Gerhard von Rad, *Old Testament Theology,* trans. D. M. G. Stalker (New York: Harper & Row, 1957), vol. 1, 239.

7 B. B. McKinney, "Let Others See Jesus in You," Copyright 1924, Renewal 1952 *Broadman Press.*

July 13, 1997

Observing the Lord's Supper Together

Background Passage: 1 Corinthians 11:2-34
Focal Passages: 1 Corinthians 11:17-22,27-34

Introduction

A misunderstanding can do great harm. For example, the ancient Romans accused the early Christian church of cannibalism! Gossip of the period claimed that the Christians ate the body of Jesus and drank His blood. The repetition of Christ's statements at the last supper probably caused this confusion. During the Lord's Supper Christians repeated Jesus' words "This is My body." And "This cup is the new covenant in My blood." Hence, the misinformed Romans wrongly concluded that all Christians were cannibals.

Charges of cannibalism are no longer brought against Christians. But the attitude of some believers causes many people to misunderstand the significance of the Lord's Supper. Frequently, we attach this ordinance to the conclusion of a worship service. Then we rush through the motions hoping it will not add too much time to the length of the service. Or we plan a personal weekend activity away from church when we will not miss too much by selecting the Sunday when the Lord's Supper is scheduled. Or more frequently, we are present and take part in the ordinance; but we have participated so many times that the Lord's Supper has become routine. Such attitudes reflect a misunderstanding of the significance of the Lord's Supper. The Lord's Supper is an important act of worship.

1 Corinthians 11:2-34
   1. Women's Participation in Worship (11:2-16)
   2. Observance of the Lord's Supper (11:17-34)

The Background

In 1 Corinthians 11:2–14:40 Paul was concerned with three distinct problems of public worship: (1) the activity of women in worship; (2) the observation of the Lord's Supper; and (3) the use of spiritual gifts. Apparently, the Corinthians had asked about the third problem for Paul wrote "Now concerning" (12:1) before he addressed the issue. But the source of his information on the first and second problem is unclear.

Corinthian women took part in the worship services. They led in prayer and addressed the congregation. Some of the more emancipated women had removed their veils when they prayed or spoke. Paul pointed out that their removal contradicted the practice of Christian women in every other church.

At Corinth the Lord's Supper was observed after a fellowship meal. However, rather than showing Christian love at the fellowship meal the Corinthians misused the occasion. Wealthy members ate all the food and became drunk. Poorer members often were left out of the fellowship meal altogether. Such behavior destroyed the unity symbolized in the Lord's Supper.

The Lesson Passage

1. Women's Participation in Worship (11:2-16)

1 Corinthians 11:2-16 is a difficult passage to understand. It pertains to the role of social customs in worship during the first century at Corinth. Specifically, the issue concerned the necessity for women to wear veils while they prayed in public. In Roman society during the first century a woman's position was changing dramatically. But both Jewish and Greek cultures had long established etiquette for women's behavior. Apparently, in their new freedom in Christ some women at Corinth had defied convention and discarded their veils while they prayed in public. Such behavior clashed with the accepted standards of the local Greek culture. Therefore, Paul admonished the women in the church to apply the principle of the stronger yielding to the weaker to this situation as well. Freedom should not be used to disrupt the church.

Shaving a woman's hair was a public mark of disgrace. And the absence of a veil in Corinth denoted that a woman was a prostitute.[1] Therefore, the issue may have been a local and temporary problem. In the minds of the local population, the absence of veils may have associated these church members with the immoral behavior of area prostitutes. Thus, their witness for Christ was compromised.

The term "head" (11:3) refers to a relationship of authority. It does not imply superiority. The New Testament conclusively states that there is equality of nature between the Father and the Son (John 1:1). Likewise, in Christ equality exists between the sexes (Gal. 3:28).

The issue of veils served as an introduction to Paul's discussion of the Lord's Supper. The discarding of veils and the abuse of both the fellowship meal and the Lord's Supper illustrated a lack of Christian unity. Women had not removed their veils in any church but Corinth. Thus the action detached the Corinthians from a universal Christian custom. Likewise, the division during the Lord's Supper was unique to Corinth.

Paul began the passage on veils with a word of commendation (11:2). Therefore, it may only have been a minor issue. In contrast, he condemned the Corinthians for their behavior in the Lord's Supper (11:17). Clearly, it was the more serious offense and one Paul obviously believed needed addressing.

2. Observance of the Lord's Supper (11:17-34)

At Corinth the Lord's Supper was observed in conjunction with a fellowship meal. This banquet was known as a "love feast" (Jude 12). It was similar to our covered-dish dinner. Each participant brought food to the meal.[2] The pattern for public festivals among both Jews and Greeks was to put all the food together for everyone to share.[3] In this way everybody would receive equal share; no one would go back to his or her home hungry.

Paul first denounced the Corinthians because of their conduct at this love feast (11:17-22). Next, he related the origin of the Lord's Supper and its significance for the bread of the Presence (11:23-26). Finally, Paul warned the Corinthians about the dangers of abusing the ordinance (11:27-34).

Verse 17: *But in giving this instruction, I do not praise you, because you come together not for the better but for the worse.*

The phrase **In giving this instruction** is a participle in the Greek text. The verb is used in the Synoptic Gospels to denote a word of command from Jesus in His authority as the Christ. Paul's use of the term signified that the authority of Christ had been imparted to him.[4] Thus the occurrence of the phrase here indicates how concerned Paul was about the abuses during the Lord's Supper. Paul was not making a few academic observations. By the authority of Christ he demanded that the Corinthians' behavior at the Supper be corrected immediately! The nature of the meal *required* an attitude of worship.

Paul censured his readers because their behavior in worship was unacceptable. He suggested that they would be better off not to attend church! Their observance of the Lord's Supper did not edify or unify the Corinthian congregation. Rather, their behavior disrupted and divided the fellowship.

Genuine worship experiences enrich both the worshiper and the church. They should always be times of celebrating Christ and His gracious provision of salvation through His death and resurrection.

Verse 18: *For, in the first place, when you come together as a church, I hear that divisions exist among you; and in part I believe it.*

The **divisions** Paul mentioned here were not the same as those presented in chapter 1.The divisions here were between the rich and the poor members of the congregation. Nonetheless, the effect was the same. The unity of the congregation was destroyed. ***And in part, I believe it*** indicated that Paul believed some exaggeration appeared in the reports he had heard about these divisions. Still Paul knew that the Lord's Supper had become a source of dissension in Corinth.

Distinctions such as wealth or social standing have no place in the Christian community. All people should be treated the same. Superior attitudes and class distinction have no proper place in the body of Christ. Nonetheless, providing the affluent better treatment is a common error. Corinth was not the only congregation in the first century to succumb to partiality (see James 2:1-13). Christians need to resist the temptation to favor individuals because of their affluence.

Verse 19: *For there must also be factions among you, so that those who are approved may become evident among you.*

Factions refers to small cliques that pridefully isolated themselves from the rest of the congregation. Such groups break a church body into narrow-minded little factions, each pursuing its own self-centered agenda. Whenever factions appear, the membership no longer can sustain a common goal for the church. The factions compete against each other. As a result energy and effort are diverted to unimportant and even sinful goals.

Paul consoled himself, however, with one small glimmer of hope about the Corinthians' situation. The contrast between proper Christian behavior and that of the factions would be apparent. The disagreement would distinguish the genuine believers from the counterfeit Christians.

Verse 20: *Therefore when you meet together, it is not to eat the Lord's Supper,*

Paul boldly declared that the ritual meal eaten at Corinth was not the Lord's Supper! Regardless of its label, the actions of the church membership made the Lord's Supper something else.

The **Lord's Supper** is a memorial meal that celebrates Jesus' sacrificial death for the sin of humanity. The Greek word rendered **the Lord's** only occurs here and in Revelation 1:10. The word stresses the close connection the meal has with the Lord. After about A.D. 100 some Christians began to call this meal the *Eucharist,* a Greek term meaning "thanksgiving." Calling the Lord's Supper the Eucharist probably arose from Jesus' giving of thanks when He gave the disciples the bread and the cup (Mark 14:22). Today, the Lord's Supper frequently is called Communion because of Paul's reference to fellowship. Whatever the name, it commemorates Jesus' death on the cross. Therefore, every aspect of its observance must reflect this truth.

When the church in Corinth assembled for the Lord's Supper, the members did not display reverent worship of God. Nor was Christian love expressed between members of the congregation. The conduct of the Corinthians nullified the spiritual meaning of the Lord's Supper. Division, not unity in Christ, was the result of their eating together.

Verse 21: *for in your eating each one takes his own supper first; and one is hungry and another is drunk.*

Evidently, the wealthy members of the church arrived early and placed a vast fare on the table. Then they stuffed themselves. Some even became intoxicated! The poorer members worked longer hours and therefore came later in the day. Their financial status did not permit them to bring adequate food. Common courtesy suggested that the prosperous members would supply an overabundance. Then there would be plenty for everybody. But when the poor arrived at church all the food already had been eaten. When the time to celebrate the Lord's Supper arrived, some members were stuffed and **drunk.** Others were sober and **hungry.**

Verse 22: *What! Do you not have houses in which to eat and drink? Or do you despise the church of God and shame those who have nothing? What shall I say to you? Shall I praise you? In this I will not praise you.*

One's private residence is the appropriate place to enjoy one's prosperity. Any exhibition of affluence at the church ridicules the central purpose of the church. The church is composed of those individuals who have been saved by the grace of God through faith in Jesus Christ. All were sinners doomed to an eternity of separation from God. Without hope, they were helpless to prevent the consequence of their own conduct. But because of His great love, God provided salvation through the death and resurrection of Christ. Thus their present status is the result of divine grace, not merit. Therefore, Christians share a common background and future. Actions which might humiliate impoverished Christians are unsuitable in the church. They contradict God's love.

The gluttony of the rich shunned the poor. Presumably, the snub caused resentment on the part of the poor. Because the Corinthians behaved in such an unsatisfactory manner, Paul refused to **praise** them. Evidently, the Corinthians expected Paul to do so.

In 11:23-26 Paul presented the historical tradition describing the institution of the Lord's Supper. He probably learned the account of the last supper at the outset of his Christian experience. Paul may have either acquired knowledge of the Lord's Supper on his visit to Jerusalem or from participation in the Lord's Supper at Damascus. His assertion that he learned it "from the Lord" emphasizes that the crucified and exalted Lord is the true source of all Christian truth and activity.

The purpose of the Lord's Supper is for participants to remember

Jesus' death as an actual event in history. Both the words and the act recall the circumstances and results of the cross. Jesus gathered with his twelve disciples to celebrate the Passover. During the course of the evening, He took bread and blessed it. He then broke the loaf and passed bread to those present. His words marked the bread as a symbol of His death. Likewise, He took the cup and after blessing it, identified the cup with a new covenant established through His death. He charged His followers to repeat this ordinance as a way to remember Him. Later that night He was arrested. He had been betrayed by one of the twelve, Judas Iscariot. The following morning Jesus was crucified.

Whenever we gather at the Lord's table, our attention should focus on the sacrificial death of Jesus and our relationship to Him. The bread is a reminder that Jesus died for us. The cup is a reminder that Jesus' death established a new covenant and freed us from sin.

The death of Christ cannot be separated from His resurrection. The same Christ who instituted the Lord's Supper before His death is alive today. He promised to come again in triumph. Therefore, to remember His death is to anticipate His return. Every time we remember Him through the Lord's Supper, we announce the hope of our faith.

Verse 27: *Therefore whoever eats the bread or drinks the cup of the Lord in an unworthy manner, shall be guilty of the body and the blood of the Lord.*

In verses 23-25 Paul recalled the words of Jesus regarding the Lord's Supper. In verse 26 he pointed out the significance and the meaning of participating in the Supper. In verses 27-34 he taught the Corinthians the proper way they should observe the Lord's Supper.

The word *therefore* stresses the consequence of what was just said. Because the Supper is a solemn rite instituted by Jesus, it must be observed with deep respect.

The root word for the adverb *unworthy* means "tipping the scales," or "bringing up the other beam of the scales."[5] The adverb is a compound of this root and the negative prefix. Thus the word denotes a scale being tipped out of balance. Actions and attitudes that reflect irreverence toward the Lord's death must never be a part of one's sharing in the Lord's Supper.

In a sense every person who comes to the Lord's table comes unworthily because all who do come can never be worthy of God's grace in Christ. There is another sense, however, that one *can* come in a worthy manner, that is, in faith, in reverence, in love, and commitment.

How does a person come to the Lord's table in an unworthy manner? One way is to believe that it gives the participant merit before God, meaning that the ceremony saves rather than the sacrifice it represents. Another way is to come without serious participation, meaning that one simply goes through the motions but with no thanksgiving, rejoicing, or meditation on the worth of Christ. To come with anything less than the highest thoughts of God and the deepest reverence for Christ is to participate in an unworthy manner.

The Lord's Supper is not a routine ceremony. It is a holy ordinance instituted by the Lord Himself. To treat the Lord's Supper otherwise is to profane the **body and blood of the Lord.** Taking the Lord's Supper in an **unworthy manner** makes that participant **guilty** of sin and disputes the results of Christ's death. He died to save people from their sin, and people should share in the Lord's Supper with a holy life.

To burn one's national flag is not an act of contempt for a piece of cloth, but an act of dishonor toward the nation the flag represents. In a similar way the bread and cup represent the sacrifice of Jesus for us. Treating the Lord's Supper irreverently, then, is to mock and to treat indifferently the One who died for our salvation.

Verse 28: *But a man must examine himself, and in so doing he is to eat of the bread and drink of the cup.*

To avoid sharing in the Lord's Supper in an unworthy manner, Christians are responsible to investigate their own lives The word **examine** is a technical term for official testing. The adjective refers to a person or object that has been tested. The word particularly was used of testing the purity and value of metals.[6] Before participation in the Lord's Supper, believers should conduct a rigorous self-examination. Attitudes and motives toward the Communion service itself, toward Christ, and toward His people should come under close inspection. If sin is know to be present, believers must turn away from their sin immediately. Then God will enable His people to celebrate rightly the Lord's Supper. The table of the Lord, indeed, is a special time and place for the believer to purify his or her life, forsaking all that might displease God.

Verses 29-30: *For he who eats and drinks, eats and drinks judgment to himself if he does not judge the body rightly. 30 For this reason many among you are weak and sick, and a number sleep.*

The sense of the verse is that one who eats without examining his or her life correctly, or eats as if at an ordinary meal, brings about his or her own **judgment.** Paul does not mean the person is eternally damned. The Bible teaches that the believer has been delivered from eternal judgment because of the death of Christ (Rom. 8:1). The judgment is, rather, God's punishment for regarding the Lord's Supper as something less than it is. The responsibility for this judgment rests, not with God, but wholly on the guilty person.

In order to avoid personal judgment, the person must properly respond to the holiness of the Supper. He or she should, according to Paul's instruction, **judge the body rightly**. The word **judge** means to distinguish, to discern. In this verse Paul meant that the believer should discern the body of Christ, that is, distinguish the Lord's Supper as different from other ordinary meals.

If the believer fails to do so, spiritual misconduct may have physical consequences. Paul stated that the reason for the ill health of some members of the Corinthian congregation was their conduct at the Lord's Supper. *Weak and sick* shows that even though God does not eternally condemn the believer who abuses the Lord's Supper, He still may punish a believer with severe illness. *Sleep* was a Christian symbol for death. Some of those who had abused the the Lord's Supper even died as a result! That which God designates as holy must be handled with reverence and respect.

Some Bible scholars view the judgment of verse 30 as spiritual rather than physical. In this view the words *weak and sick* and *sleep* refer to one's soul and not to one's body. The judgment, then, would be that those who abuse the Lord's table cannot understand the significance and true nature of the Lord's Supper. Consequently, they cannot participate in it in a true sense. And those who have fallen asleep have done so spiritually, that is, they have ceased to participate in the Lord's Supper altogether.

Verse 31: *But if we judged ourselves rightly, we would not be judged.*

Apparently, the Corinthians failed to recognize that they had a problem. Their self-evaluation failed to reveal their sins. Therefore, the Corinthians' conclusion was the opposite of God's. Because they acted irreverently at the Lord's Supper, God would judge them.

Had the Corinthians, on the other hand, judged themselves *rightly* they would not have been judged by God. In other words, if the believers at Corinth had distinguished between what they were and what they should have been, they would not have received God's judgment. Had they truly discovered what their lives were like, they could have made positive adjustments and avoided judgment

Verse 32: *But when we are judged, we are disciplined by the Lord so that we will not be condemned along with the world.*

The calamity that had fallen those who were objects of God's judgment was a token of His love for them. The purpose of His judgment was to prevent them from sharing in the condemnation of the world.

Verse 33: *So then, my brethren, when you come together to eat, wait for one another.*

At this point Paul concluded the matter about the Lord's Super. He urged them to *wait for one another* before they began eating. Waiting for everyone to gather reflects a respect for each individual member. To await any individual is to declare that person significant enough that the body is incomplete without his or her presence. If a believer is so hungry and so undisciplined that he or she cannot wait, Paul had, not a suggestion, but a command for the believer to follow.

Verse 34: *If anyone is hungry, let him eat at home, so that you will not come together for judgment. The remaining matters I will arrange when I come.*

Physical appetites should be satisfied prior to going to church. Otherwise, the spiritual condition will not be strengthened. The purpose of genuine worship is spiritual, not physical.

Paul's statement **the remaining matters I will arrange when I come** indicates that he did not know when he would return to Corinth. Thus these other matters were not urgent. Still, they would receive his attention when he arrived.

For Further Study

1. Read "A Woman's Place in the First Century" in the Winter 1991 issue of the *Biblical Illustrator.*

2. Read about the Love Feast in the *Holman Bible Dictionary,* pages 898-899 or in another Bible dictionary.

3. Examine your attitude during several worship experiences. Consider ways to improve your worship experiences in the future.

1 Brown, "1 Corinthians," *Broadman Bible Commentary,* vol. 10, 53.

2 Morris, *First Corinthians,* Tyndale New Testament Commentary, 158.

3 Mare, "1 Corinthians," *Expositor's Bible Commentary,* vol. 10, 259.

4 *Theological Dictionary of the New Testament,* 1967 ed., παραγγέω" by Otto Schmitz, 5:761-65.

5 *Dictionary of New Testament Theology,* 1978 ed., "Right" by Erich Tiedtks, 3:348; *Theological Dictionary of the New Testament,* 1964 ed., "ἄξιοσ" by Werner Forester, 1:379.

6 *Theological Dictionary of the New Testament,* 1964 ed., "δοκιμάζω" by Walter Grundmann, 2:255-56.

July 20, 1997

Understanding My Place in the Church

Background Passage: 1 Corinthians 12:1-31a
Focal Passages: 1 Corinthians 12:12-15,18-27

Introduction

Church members frequently feel unimportant. They believe their contribution to the church is insignificant. In reality, however, every member is important. Each has a unique role in the congregation. That every member has a ministry can be seen at a typical Sunday morning worship service. The role and significance of the pastor and minister of music are obvious. The same is true of the choir members.

Have you ever stopped to consider the other people who make the worship hour possible by their faithful services? Some of these servants are rarely seen making their contribution. For instance, the sanctuary is cleaned each week. The heating or air conditioning maintains a comfortable temperature inside regardless of the temperature on the outside. The bulletin with its order of service is typed and distributed on Sunday. Repairs to equipment, furniture, and the building are routinely made. Flowers provide an extra touch of beauty to the space. Finally, the building is unlocked so that all may go in and worship.

Walking to the place of worship, several people smile and speak to you. As you enter the sanctuary the ushers greet you, give you the bulletin, and offer to assist you in finding a seat. After you are seated you look around to see who is present. Perhaps you note several small children scampering to get seated before their mothers reprimand them. On the back pew two teenage girls are giggling softly. Toward the front an elderly couple sits like statues, staring at the empty pulpit. They have been faithful members for over 50 years. For a moment that thought causes you to reflect on the changes in the church during that time. But the entrance of a young couple interrupts your reflection. You presume that their newborn baby must be in the nursery (where there are more people serving you may never see). All of these individuals strengthen your church.

Church is one of the very few places we go where every age group is welcome. Together they give the congregation a special existence. The younger ages contribute life and vitality. The older generations offer maturity and wisdom. The result is heard and felt as the congregation stands to sing. All the voices unite in praise. Each voice is unique, but together they produce a beautiful sound.

Although various members perform different functions, they are all vital to the total work of the church. Every Christian is important. Each possesses a special gift from God. It is critical that each person fills the place God has assigned him or her.

1 Corinthians 12:1-31a

1. One Spirit, Many Gifts (12:1-11)
2. One Body, Many Members (12:12-14)
3. No Member Unnecessary (12:15-17)
4. Each Member Placed by God (12:18-20)
5. No Member Self-Sufficient (12:21-26)
6. Each One a Member of the Body (12:27-31a)

The Background

Misunderstandings about spiritual gifts created problems in Corinth. Some within the congregation expressed religious pride because of their spiritual gifts and formed elitist groups. Members were judgmental of those they perceived as being less spiritual. Some felt that they had superior gifts and, consequently, looked down on others who did not have their gifts.[1]

Although 1 Corinthians 12:1–14:40 is divided by chapters in English Bibles, it was a single unit in Paul's letter. In 12:1-31a the apostle argued that although a variety of spiritual gifts existed at Corinth, they should bring about unity in the church. In 12:31b–13:13 Paul declared that love was a better method for achieving unity among the believers: "I show you a still more excellent way" (12:31b). In 14:1-25 Paul discussed the proper usage of the spiritual gifts.

Although Paul changed topics at 15:1 ("Now I make known to you"), the new topic is not unrelated to the discussion on spiritual gifts. The gospel is superior even to the greatest spiritual gift. It is "of first importance" (15:3). Thus this entire section of Paul's message rises to the climax of Christ's resurrection and the believers' resurrection (15:1-58). The ultimate unity of the church is found in its hope of resurrection.

The Lesson Passage

1. One Spirit, Many Gifts (12:1-11)

Again, Paul emphasized that he was writing to fellow believers. He addressed them as "brethren." Among the questions asked by the

Corinthians was one concerning spiritual gifts. The question they had on their mind was something like, "Is a spiritual gift the mark of spirituality?"[2] Not wishing his readers to be uninformed on this important issue, the apostle launched into a lengthy exposition.

Because misunderstanding spiritual gifts was at the heart of the problem in Corinth, Paul focused on the work of the Holy Spirit in believers. He refuted the exclusive claim of the so-called spiritual Corinthians at Corinth. They bragged that they alone possessed the Holy Spirit. This claim was established on their experiences with certain spectacular gifts. The Holy Spirit in a believer, however, is proof of God's presence no matter what spiritual gifts a believer has.

Paul appealed to the most fundamental Christian experience to prove his point. Salvation is an act of divine grace. The simplest confession of salvation is "Jesus is Lord" (12:3). This confession is evidence of the Spirit's presence. The Spirit points people to Jesus. One who was under the inspiration of the Holy Spirit could never curse Jesus.

Spiritual gifts are the result of the indwelling of the Holy Spirit. Six times in verses 7-11, Paul stated that the Holy Spirit gives the spiritual gifts. The spiritual gifts are for the common good of the entire congregation. They are not given to benefit one individual at the expense of others. These gifts enable the whole church to perform the ministry of Christ in the present age. The church is the extension of the life of Christ in the world today. Therefore, Christians do not select the spiritual gift that they want. Rather, the Holy Spirit determines the gift the Christian needs to best serve the body.

2. One Body, Many Members (12:12-14)

Paul illustrated the nature of the Christian community by comparing it to the human body. Individual members of the church are like the variety of organs that compose the physical body.

Verse 12: *For even as the body is one and yet has many members, and all the members of the body, though they are many, are one body, so also is Christ.*

The human body is composed of many individual parts, each of which has importance, but the whole body functions as a single unit. It cannot be subdivided into many bodies. If the body is divided, the part that is cut off dies; and the rest of the body loses some of its effectiveness. The human body is more than the total of all its parts.

The human body is even more complex than Paul could have imagined. The adult human body contains 17-20 square feet of skin, 5 million individual hairs, approximately 650 muscles, over 100 joints, 206 bones, and 50,000 miles of blood vessels and capillaries! An average weight body contains 79 pints of water and 11 pints of blood. For supporting weight, human bone is stronger than granite. A block the size of a matchbox can support ten tons. The nerves in the ear are so sensitive that the inner ear contains no blood vessels. Otherwise, a person would be deafened by the sound of the body's own pulse.[3]

Christ's body is also one. While there may be many religious denominations, there is only one body of Christ; and all believers belong to it. To stress this truth, Paul abruptly remarked **so also is Christ.** This conclusion directed the reader's attention from the human illustration to the spiritual truth. Paul did not identify the church by name. The church is the body of Christ, and, therefore, is to exhibit the identity and nature of Christ. Moreover, by this statement Paul referred to Christ as the church, showing the complete unity of Christ with His church.

Verses 13-14: *For by one Spirit we were all baptized into one body, whether Jews or Greeks, whether slaves or free, and we were all made to drink of one Spirit. 14 For the body is not one member, but many.*

The stress of verse 13 explicitly is on the corporate work of the Holy Spirit. He creates unity in the church by incorporating all believers into a single body. Racial and social distinctions disappear in the unity of the body of Christ.

Baptized denotes the baptism of the Holy Spirit. This occurs at conversion. Paul's reference to baptism may also have reminded the Corinthians of their water baptism. be intended to recall the water baptism of the readers. If so **to drink of one Spirit** may refer to the Lord's Supper.

Paul, however, did not mean that the baptism of the Holy Spirit and water baptism are the same. Water baptism is a public testimony both to the church and to the world of one's faith in Christ. It is a visible, physical ordinance done to believers by another believer in obedience to Jesus' commandment (Matt. 28:19). The Holy Spirit's baptizing work, on the other hand, is the work of God, not man, that immerses the one who believes on Christ into His body, the church.

Verse 13 is the last reference to the Holy Spirit in this chapter. It is a reference to receiving the Holy Spirit, not to the gifts of the Holy Spirit. At conversion one is baptized by the Holy Spirit into Christ's body, and the Spirit becomes a permanent resident in one's life. His presence unites every believer into Christ's body, yet each believer maintains an individuality of his or her own. Like a body, the church has numerous ,distinct organs. Each member has a special function in the body.

3. No Member Unnecessary (12:15-17)

Every organ or member of the physical body is necessary for the body to perform correctly. Paul used the significance of each member of the human body to illustrate the importance of each individual Christian in Christ's body. Some believers may perform more important tasks, but all believers are vital to the whole body.

Verse 15: *If the foot says, "Because I am not a hand, I am not a part of the body," it is not for this reason any the less a part of the body.*

One of the less attractive parts of the human body is **the foot.** It is the most distant from the head. In contrast **the hand** is one of those body parts that is unique because many of the tasks people perform require the special capabilities of the human hand. Hands are often embellished with rings and nail polish. While feet too may be decorated with nail polish, they usually are covered by shoes. The hands can be moved to touch any location on one's body. But the feet have an extremely restricted range on most people. How many people can touch the top of their head with their toes? Nonetheless, the feet are not **any the less a part of the body.** Indeed, without the feet human mobility is impeded. Without the feet even the ability to stand upright would not be possible.

The questions in verse 17 point out the absolute need for diversity. The eye can neither hear nor smell. An ear and a nose are necessary to perform those tasks. What is true of the human body is also true of Christ's body. Spiritually gifted people make their unique contribution to the whole body.

4. Each Member Placed by God (12:18-20)

God is sovereign over the church. Therefore, He determines the placement of each individual gift in the church.

Verse 18: *But now God has placed the members, each one of them, in the body, just as He desired.*

Spiritual gifts are not natural talents. Spiritual gifts are special abilities for ministry people receive at conversion, not at physical birth, in order to serve God's purposes. Spiritual gifts have their roots in the Old Testament. Old Testament Scriptures teach that God was active in the events of history, especially those involving the people He claimed for His own possession, the Israelites. Frequently, God's work was accomplished through individuals He chose to perform specific tasks. This tradition continued in the New Testament. When Christ began His ministry, He selected twelve disciples, whom He commissioned (less Judas Iscariot) to continue His ministry after He departed.

Those whom God has placed in His body as members also have been given a spiritual gift to serve the church and the world. To be discontent with one's place in Christ's body is to question God and imply that He does not know best! Worse, it is to rebel against God and His decisions about the body of Christ. How much better for the Christian to thank God for his or her gift and to use the gifts and the opportunities God has given.

Verses 19-20: *If they were all one member, where would the body be? 20 But now there are many members, but one body.*

The initial eleven disciples were a dissimilar group. Peter, Andrew, James, and John were Galilean fishermen. Matthew was a tax-collector for the Romans. Simon the Zealot was a political insurgent.

Later disciples were even more diverse. Paul received a formal education in religion. Luke was a physician. Onesimus was a runaway slave (Phil. 10). Lydia presumably owned and operated her own commercial enterprise (Acts 16:14). But each one contributed to the growth of the church. By the action of the Holy Spirit, an individual Christian is made one with all other believers who make up the body of Christ.

5. No Member Self-Sufficient (12:21-26)

In the previous passage Paul encouraged those members of the church who had received the less spectacular gifts. Having demonstrated their importance to the whole body, he then turned his attention to those members in the church with the greater gifts. Some of these prideful believers had aggravated the divisiveness in the church by their arrogance. They bragged that they did not need other members who had what they perceived to be lesser gifts.

Verse 21: *And the eye cannot say to the hand, "I have no need of you"; or again the head to the feet, "I have no need of you."*

Christians sometimes boast of their independence. They claim that they can live a Christian life on their own. They do not need help from anyone else, they say. Paul addressed such thinking in this passage. If there were no hand, he pointed out, then hand and eye coordination for accomplishing creative tasks would be nonexistent. For another example, a person might decide to move, but without the body's feet the body cannot change locations.

Verse 22: *On the contrary, it is much truer that the members of the body which seem to be weaker are necessary;*

The word **weaker** means "without strength, feeble sick." The emphasis of the term is on the perceived unimportance of these members.[4] The descriptive word probably was used by those in Corinth who considered themselves more spiritual than other believers. God composed the body so that the organs do not compete with one another over superiority. Rather, they complement each other and form a wholeness. That is the way the church should function as well. Whenever any one organ ceases to function, the whole body suffers.

Verse 23: *and those members of the body which we deem less honorable, on these we bestow more abundant honor, and our unseemly members come to have more abundant seemliness,*

On one occasion James and John came to Jesus and requested a position of honor in the kingdom of God (Mark 10:37). Jesus responded by declaring that the kingdom of God differed from earthly nations. In His kingdom "whoever wishes to become great among you shall be your servant; and whoever wishes to be first among you shall be slave of all" (Mark 10:43-44).

Verse 24: *whereas our seemly members have no need of it. But God has so composed the body, giving more abundant honor to that member which lacked,*

Giving honor to the spectacular or strong is humanity's custom. God, however, honors the weak. Whenever the church conforms to God's will, it honors those whom God honors. Those who have impressive gifts have no need to seek acclaim because their role in the church gives them a certain prestige. But those with the less glamorous tasks frequently require assurance that they are contributing to the harmony and benefit of the whole.

Verse 25: *so that there may be no division in the body, but that the members may have the same care for one another.*

The church requires the mutual care of all members. The interdependence of believers should foster accord, not discord. Discord is wrong and damaging and causes the body to stop working correctly. In the physical body, when organs cease to function properly, the body becomes ill. When left untreated, the body becomes more incapacitated and may even die. The same is true in the spiritual sphere. While schisms can never destroy the body of Christ, they can ruin its health and usefulness.

Verse 26: *And if one member suffers, all the members suffer with it; if one member is honored, all the members rejoice with it.*

Empathy was absent in Corinth. Issues such as eating meat sacrificed to idols (1 Cor. 8:1-13; 10:14-22) and problems such as the scandal at the Lord's Supper (1 Cor. 10:21; 11:17-34) reflected contempt by some members for the needs of other believers.

Infection in a small organ produces a fever that racks the entire physical body. If an organ, such as one of the lungs, becomes diseased, medical doctors do not remove the lung and hospitalize it alone. The entire person becomes the patient. The same is true of the church. One member who has stopped exercising his or her gift for the good of the church, affects the whole body.

6. Each One a Member of the Body (12:27-31a)

In this passage Paul put particular emphasis on God's organization of the body of Christ. God determines the gift one receives. Likewise, He appoints the gifted individual to a specific place of service.

Verse 27: *Now you are Christ's body, and individually members of it.*

God's plan for the believer involves both the uniqueness of the individual and the combined strength of the whole church. As the church understands the unity of the body and the necessity of all members, the Spirit empowers it through the complementary nature of the gifts. As individual members exercise their unique gift, they mature spiritually and the whole body grows.

This passage was a corrective for an error on the part of the Corinthian believers. They considered the spiritual gifts that drew the most attention to the individual to be the most desirable. Paul, however, refuted their pride. He concluded that those gifts that promote the common good are the ones to be more desired by the believers.

For Further Study

1. Read "The Gifts of the Holy Spirit" in the Fall 1991 issue of the *Biblical Illustrator.*

2. Read about spiritual gifts in the *Holman Bible Dictionary,* pages 1300-1301, or in another Bible dictionary.

3. Paul emphasized the importance of every Christian. Seek to discover your spiritual gift. Investigate ways to use this gift in your church. Remember that exercising your gift will edify your church.

-----

1 David W. Perkins, "Superspiritually in Corinth," *The Theological Educator 14* (Fall 1983), 41-42.

2 Kenneth S. Hemphill, Spiritual Gifts: *Empowering the New Testament Church* (Nashville: Broadman Press, 1988), 54.

3 Edmund H. Harvey, Jr., *Reader's Digest Book of Facts* (Pleasantville, New York: Reader's Digest Association, 1987), 194-96.

4 Morris, *First Corinthians, Tyndale New Testament Commentary,* 176.

July 27, 1997

Expressing Love in All We Do

Background Passage: 1 Corinthians 12:31b–13:13
Focal Passages: 1 Corinthians 12:31b–13:13

Introduction

Early in his ministry Dwight L. Moody envisioned God as standing behind the sinner with a double-edged sword ready to strike at the slightest provocation. He used the Scripture as a weapon to frighten his congregation or for texts to prove his opinions. In his preaching Moody tended to stress God's judgment on sinners more than God's love for sinners. An event happened in his life, however, that changed his preaching

One evening Moody heard Harry Moorhouse preach. Moorhouse had been a prizefighter, pickpocket, and alcoholic. After his conversion he became a popular preacher. His text that night was John 3:16. "For God so loved the world, that He gave His only begotten Son, that whoever believes in Him shall not perish, but have eternal life." For the first time in his ministry, Moody began to understand the depth of God's love for sinners. A marked change took place in his life. He spent weeks studying every passage in the Bible on God's love. Then Moody's preaching ministry began to reveal his own deep love for Christ, and His preaching showed his own compassion for people. The love of God became his only motivation for ministry. Moody related that God's love was the one thing above all else that draws people to Him.[1]

Love continues to be the basic need in our world. But what is love? Amid his discussion on spiritual gifts, Paul defined the concept of divine love. 1 Corinthians 13 has become a classic. We memorize it early in life, yet we tend to forget its meaning. Each word and phrase is packed with significance.

1 Corinthians 12:31b–13:13

1. The Priority of Love (12:31b–13:3)
2. The Practice of Love (13:4-7)
3. The Permanence of Love (13:8-12)
4. The Preeminence of Love (13:13)

The Background

Chapter 13 bridges two passages on the problem of spiritual gifts (12:1-31 and 14:1-25). The Corinthians' misunderstanding of the purposes of spiritual gifts was partly to blame for the divisions in the church. So Paul sought to put spiritual gifts into the proper perspective. Although spiritual gifts were necessary and wonderful, they were to be exercised in a spirit of love. Also, Paul pointed out that spiritual gifts will someday fade away. Only faith, hope, and love will endure. Of those three, Paul said, the greatest is love.

God's own love for the Corinthians was the basis of the Christian community's existence. The church had come into being through God's love as expressed in His Son. The church was sustained in love as its members exercised toward others the love they had experienced from God. Unity, not division, would have been the result if the Corinthians had made love their ambition rather than fostering personal pride because of spiritual gifts.

The Lesson Passage

1. The Priority of Love (12:31b–13:3)

Verse 31b: *And I show you a still more excellent way.*

Although spiritual gifts are important, Paul pointed out that to be effective they must be used in a spirit of love. Gifts used without demonstrating love for others are meaningless and fruitless.

Verse 31b is a transitional statement between Paul's reflections on spiritual gifts and his consideration of love. He concluded the section on gifts by exhorting his readers to "earnestly desire the greater gifts." Next Paul moved to a *still more excellent way.* Love is not a spiritual gift. It is superior to the highest of the gifts. It is a way (or a path), which was an ancient Jewish idiom for the course of one's life. Love is the primary means of living in God's design for humanity. This way of life is within the reach of the most ordinary Christian. Paul assumed if his readers recognized the preeminence of love, they would strive to show love to *all* believers.

Verse 1: *If I speak with the tongues of men and of angels, but do not have love, I have become a noisy gong or a clanging cymbal.*

If indicates that the condition which follows is a hypothetical possibility. *The tongues of men and of angels* certainly refers to the gift of tongues (12:10,28,30). Nonetheless, the language is general enough to apply to all speech. Eloquent discourse can be as much a source of vanity as ecstatic speech.

In verses 2-3 Paul exaggerated his point to show the preeminence of love. Using examples from life, he pressed the point to the extreme. Speech, even ecstatic speech, even the language of angels, he said, is worthless without love. Paul, of course, was being hypothetical when he wrote about tongues of angels. The Bible does not indicate that the angels of God speak a language humans could learn. In all the occurrences of angels speaking to men and women in the Bible, angels spoke without exception in the language of the person or persons they addressed. So Paul meant that even if he spoke with the eloquence of the greatest of orators, even with angelic eloquence, he would only be a **noisy gong or a clangning cymbal.** The loftiest truth spoken by the world's best orator falls short if the truth is spoken without love.

The Corinthian believers needed to hear Paul's words. Their pride in the gift of languages resulted in selfishness and arrogance, not in seeking to serve others. Without love what they thought was the most important gift amounted to nothing more than gibberish and babble.

In Paul's day the Greek language had several words for love. The most common word was *philos,* which was the general term for affection, love, friendship, devotion, and so forth. The word *eros* designated the love between man and woman, especially involving sensual desire and sexual passion. The word *agape* was often used as a synonym and placed beside the other two words for emphasis.[2] The writers of the New Testament used *agape* to denote the exclusive love commanded by Jesus. Thereafter, the word was defined by the love Jesus Himself exhibited, particularly in His death on the cross (John 3:16).

Agape **love** reveals the very nature of God. Also, love should be the basis for the relationship of one believer to every other believer. A person who hates another believer cannot be a genuine Christian. Because God is love, a person's failure to love can only mean that he or she has no true knowledge of God, has not really been born of God, and therefore does not have God's nature (1 John 4:20-21). The exhibition of love towards other Christians provides the world verification of one's commitment to Jesus (John 13:35). Authentic love is not passive but manifests its presence in action (1 John 3:18).

The **noisy gong** was a type of loud percussion instrument, perhaps like a cymbal.[3] Paul probably had in mind the noise made in pagan worship as metal instruments were struck. Israelites used the **cymbal** in worship at the temple. Both instruments made loud, echoing sounds. Paul asserted that the best speech, if the motivation was not love, was nothing but noise!

Verse 2: *If I have the gift of prophecy, and know all mysteries and all knowledge; and if I have all faith, so as to remove mountains, but do not have love, I am nothing.*

Paul regarded **prophecy** as one of the greatest of the spiritual gifts. He ranked it second only to being an apostle. Prophecy is the announcement of God's word through the presence and power of the Holy Spirit.

Mysteries refers to concealed divine truths that are revealed to God's prophets. **Knowledge** points to knowledge people gather for themselves. It includes science and other academic disciplines. Together, these terms embrace all wisdom, both human and divine.

Jesus claimed that a minimum amount of faith permitted one to move mountains by merely speaking to them (Matt. 17:20). Despite the extent of one's accomplishments, however, if great attainments are not motivated by love they are worthless.

Verse 3: *And if I give all my possessions to feed the poor, and if I surrender my body to be burned, but do not have love, it profits me nothing.*

Old Testament Scriptures stressed the responsibility of God's people to care for the helpless. With the advent of Christianity, the church accepted the responsibility for helping poor members. The early church also reached a multitude of impoverished people. Jesus had taught that His followers must be willing to part with personal possessions if their sale could help the poor (Luke 12:33). Compliance with this teaching became the basis for a ruler's rejection of Him (Luke 18:22-23) and the evidence of Zaccheus's new relationship with Him (Luke 19:8).

Burning the **body** may be a reference to voluntary slavery, in which case the burning indicated branding. If this is a correct interpretation, Paul alluded to the practice of selling oneself into slavery and taking the purchase price to buy food for the poor.[4]

More likely, the reference is to martyrdom, the giving of one's life because of one's belief. Christianity had a fragile legal status in the Roman Empire. As long as it remained a sect of Judaism, Christianity enjoyed the protection of the state. After the church's separation from Judiasm, however, the new faith was considered to be an illegal religion and was persecuted by the state. Even before the final rift, the orthodox within Judaism began a campaign to repress the gospel about Jesus. On occasion the subjugation ended in the death of Christians.

If these great sacrifices were not the consequence of love, no merit exists in the martyrdom. Love is more valuable than the greatest gift and the noblest act of self-sacrifice.

2. The Practice of Love (13:4-7)

After his declaration on the merits of love, Paul described love's nature. The descriptive characteristics that follow establish love as an action. Love is not an emotional sensation only. Love expresses itself through deeds.

Verse 4: *Love is patient, love is kind and is not jealous; love does not brag and is not arrogant,*

In Ionic Greek the word translated as **patient** represented the patience and perseverance of a physician treating severe chronic illnesses.

Patience also described the steadfastness of a soldier enduring hardships until a goal was reached.[5] In the New Testament the word took on a special theological significance based on its usage in the Greek translation of the Old Testament (the Septuagint.) The Septuagint used a Greek word for a Hebrew word that literally means "long of nostrils." The Hebrew idiom usually is rendered into the English by the phrase "slow to become angry." The idiom was derived from the flared nostrils of an animal (or a person) when enraged. The expression routinely represents an attribute of God. In Exodus 34:5-8 it is one of the attributes that the Lord revealed as a manifestation of His own character. The image pictures God taking a long, deep breath as He delays His anger.

The Greek word was used by Paul in Romans 2:4 to characterize God's desire for people to repent. In the life of a Christian, patience is no mere endurance or feeble indulgence. It is a spiritual force connected to one's knowledge of God. Patience permits the Christian to endure irritations without losing one's temper. It concerns tolerance of people rather than endurance of circumstances.

The word **kind** has a moral sense in which inner greatness is joined to genuine goodness of heart. It denoted the capacity to show friendliness or kindness to everyone. The word indicated God's benevolent activity, His constant mercy and readiness to forgive sin. In the New Testament kindness is a fruit of the Holy Spirit (Gal. 5:22). The Christian must be kind without calculating the object of that kindness or without thought of reward. Whereas patience indicates a willingness to suffer without retaliation, kindness seeks to do good to the one who has wronged it.

The word **jealous** can mean "jealous" or "zealous." The former sense fits the context here better. Love does not envy the attainments or the possessions of others.

The emphasis of the word **brag** is on the rhetorical form of boasting with its element of exaggeration, offensiveness, unsettlement, and flattery. It is a baseless chatter. Bragging refers to wounds others, causing unrest and discord.[6] The term refers to the braggart who vaunts himself or herself without a basis for doing so. This is the only occurrence of the word in the New Testament. The word **arrogant** only occurs in 1 Corinthians 4:6,18-19; 5:2; 8:1 and 13:4. Whereas the word brag marks external bravado, arrogant is internal self-confidence.

Verse 5: does not act unbecomingly; it does not seek its own, is not provoked, does not take into account a wrong suffered,

Love is not ill-mannered. It is unwilling to behave boorishly or to do anything shameful to others. Love does not insist on its own way. The word **provoked** usually means "to stir to anger" or in its passive state "to be irritated" or "incensed."[7]

Human nature frequently takes pleasure in the misfortune of others, particularly one's enemies. Genuine love, however, **does not take into**

account a wrong suffered. It does not hold a grudge. Paul could appreciate this quality of the divine nature. He once devoted his life to the destruction of Christ's church, but God had saved him and forgiven him of the past. Christ's bitterest mortal foe became His greatest champion.

Verse 6: *does not rejoice in unrighteousness, but rejoices with the truth;*

Love does not find joy in the wrongdoing of others. It does not use the occasion of someone else's failure to find pride in a sense of one's own righteousness. Rather, love delights in conformity to God's will, whether by oneself or by others. Who complies to the divine will makes no difference. The joy is derived from loyalty to the truth.

Verse 7: *bears all things, believes all things, hopes all things, endures all things.*

Bears all things probably means that love makes allowances for the weakness of others. The Greek verb has the sense of "to hide by covering."[8] This sense may indicate that love is slow to expose the faults of other people. More likely, the verb points to the permanence of love. Love endures every onslaught.

In the Old Testament the mercy seat was the place where Aaron sprinkled the blood of the atonement for the ark and for the sins of the people. That mercy seat was a covering that prefigured the final covering of sin that Jesus accomplished on the cross. In the cross of Christ, God cast His great love over our sin and covered it for all those who would trust His Son. Love's nature seeks to save, to heal, to redeem.

Love **believes all things.** Love causes one to trust others. It prefers to be extravagant in trust rather than too skeptical. It elects always to give one the benefit of the doubt.

Love **hopes all things.** Love does not produce some type of unreasoning optimism. On the other hand, it never accepts defeat as being final. This hope does not rest in one's own ability; it springs from an absolute confidence in Christ.

Love **endures all things.** When love encounters disappointment, it manifests a steady fortitude. It continues to survive under the harshest and most unfavorable circumstances.

3. The Permanence of Love (13:8-12)

Paul concluded his exposition on *agape* love by comparing the permanence of love to the temporary nature of the spiritual gifts. The necessity and purpose of the gifts is restricted to one's earthly life. In contrast, love is an attribute of the unchanging, eternal God. Therefore, love cannot be confined to time and space.

Verse 8: *Love never fails; but if there are gifts of prophecy, they* *will be done away; if there are tongues, they will cease; if there is knowledge, it will be done away.*

Spiritual gifts (like prophecy, tongues, and knowledge) are of a temporal nature. They only have significance during one's worldly existence. **Prophecy** is declaring God's word. Because of the uncertainty and complexity of life, prophecy has immense value in one's lifetime. But after one is brought into the presence of God, prophecy no longer will be necessary or useful. Likewise, **tongues** and **knowledge** are useful in the present age. But in heaven they too will forfeit all of their usefulness.

Love, however, is permanent. Because it is the very essence of God's nature, love will exist as long as God exists! It will continue to function and have worth forever.

Verse 9: *For we know in part and we prophesy in part;*

Spiritual knowledge is still partial. Even though the ultimate revelation of God is the incarnation of Jesus Christ, perfect understanding of His life and work is impossible (John 21:25).

Verse 10: *but when the perfect comes, the partial will be done away.*

Paul anticipated eternity. He recognized that when the Lord returned and established His new order, a dramatic change would transpire. In the present life the limitations of physical life only allow a **partial** knowledge. At the consummation of the age, however, the inadequate and incomplete will be displaced by the unhindered closeness of Christ. All of the worldly knowledge humanity has accumulated will be of no consequence in the **perfect** presence of the exalted Christ.

Verse 11: *When I was a child, I used to speak like a child, think like a child, reason like a child; when I became a man, I did away with childish things.*

A child differs greatly from an adult. Childhood is only a brief phase of life. It is a temporary and constantly changing period. During this stage of human development, a person's mental skills remain unfinished. Thus children frequently behave in an illogical manner.

Whenever an individual reaches adulthood, physical and mental capability reaches its full potential. A different perspective on life is achieved. Activities once considered vital become silly or obsolete. For instance, childhood games may help develop motor skills in children, but they have little benefit for grown adults.

The Corinthians were acting like children because of their boasting of possessing special spiritual gifts. If they would show love instead of pride, then the Corinthians would act spiritually mature. Love reflects maturity. The time had come, Paul said, for the Christians at Corinth to do away with their immature behavior and conduct themselves like mature adults.

Verse 12: *For now we see in a mirror dimly, but then face to* face; now I know in part, but then I will know fully just as I also have been fully known.

Spiritual gifts had become the source of jealousy at Corinth because the use of gifts was motivated by selfishness. Certain Corinthians desired to prove themselves more spiritual than other church members. This self-centered attitude was distorted. It reminded Paul of gazing into a mirror. A first-century **mirror** was made of polished metal, usually bronze. The reflection had an appearance of reality. Nonetheless, it was indistinct, not presenting an accurate image. So too was the Corinthians' superspirituality. Their lives had a certain semblance of godliness, although their selfishness, like an indistinct image in an imperfect mirror, could not be detected easily.

When love motivates the use of a spiritual gift, believers will honor weaker members. Then exaltation of weaker members will lessen the differences between members and so unify the church.

Thus love was the only source of unity in the congregation at Corinth.[9] And even though love and unity in this life are imperfect, in heaven we will be face to face—relationships perfected in love.

4. The Preeminence of Love (13:13)

Before returning to a discussion on the application of the spiritual gifts, Paul summed up the supremacy of love in one penetrating declaration.

Verse 13: *But now faith, hope, love, abide these three; but the greatest of these is love.*

The word **now** does not seem to imply time here. Rather, it had the sense of "and in conclusion." Paul had completed his argument.

Big changes await God's people when they depart this life. Things such as spiritual gifts not only will lose their value, they will cease to exist completely. They no longer will have any relevance. **Faith, hope,** and agape **love** will characterize God's people in eternity.

The Corinthians esteemed certain spiritual gifts such as knowledge and speaking in tongues. Paul suggested that they wrongly judged the significance of these gifts. Other gifts such as prophecy (preaching) were more important. Then he stated that all spiritual gifts were secondary to the great qualities of faith, hope, and love. And of the three, none meant more than *agape* love.

For Further Study

1. Read about Christian love in the *Holman Bible Dictionary,* pages 896-898, or in another Bible dictionary of your choice.

2. Read "The Love of God" in the Summer 1990 issue of the *Biblical Illustrator.*

3. Read the Book of 1 John in the New Testament. Note the numerous parallels and illustrations to 1 Corinthians 13.

4. Recall a recent demonstration of your love for others. Compare and contrast your action to the characteristics of genuine Christian love as described by Paul in 1 Corinthians 13.

---

1 Paul Gericke, *Crucial Experiences in the Life of D. L. Moody* (New Orleans, Louisiana: Insight Press, 1978), 31-38.

2 *Dictionary of New Testament Theology,* 1976 ed., "Love" by Walther Günther, Hans-Georg Link, and Colin Brown, 2:538-39,547; *Theological Dictionary of the New Testament* 1964 ed., "ἀγαπάω" by Elhelbert Stauffer, 1:35-38.

3 *Holman Bible Dictionary,* 1991 ed., "Gong," 567.

4 Brown, "1 Corinthians," *Broadman Bible Commentary,* vol. 10, 371.

5 *Theological Dictionary of the New Testament,* 1967 ed., "μακροθυμία" by J. Horst, 4:375.

6 *Theological Dictionary of the New Testament,* 1968 ed., "περπερέυομαι" by Herbert Braun, 6:93-94.

7 *Theological Dictionary of the New Testament,* 1967 ed., "παροξύονω" by Heinrich Seesemann, 5:857.

8 Morris, First Corinthians, *Tyndale New Testament Commentary,* 185.

August 3, 1997

Using Spiritual Gifts Effectively

Background Passage: 1 Corinthians 14
Focal Passage: 1 Corinthians 14:12-25

Introduction

Silence filled the room. The young lady continued to stare at me. Her blank expression seemed to scream out her failure to comprehend my words. I had used every method and plan for evangelism I knew, but the empty expression on her face had never varied. In a few moments I realized she would rise up from her chair and walk out the door. She then would board an airplane and travel to a distant city. I probably would never see her again. And she might never again hear the good news that God loved her.

"God loves her!" The thought struck me like a bolt of lightning. I looked directly into her dark brown eyes and deliberately repeated the verse I had learned as a child. The words were simple yet effective. "For God so loved the world, that He gave His only begotten Son, that whoever believes in Him shall not perish, but have eternal life." I watched in amazement as a tear began to trickle down her cheek. Suddenly, her stony countenance melted beneath a river of tears. Then she glared at me in shock and asked, "Is that what you have been trying to tell me for the last hour?"

I learned a valuable lesson that day about God. Not only does He love us, but He communicates His love effectively. We need to do likewise. As we use our spiritual gifts, we need to ask ourselves if we are using them effectively?

1 Corinthians 14
1. Prophecy and Tongues Contrasted (14:1-11)
2. Superiority of Prophecy (14:12-25)
3. Need for Order in Worship (14:26-40)

The Background

In 1 Corinthians 14 Paul returned to his discussion of spiritual gifts. He previously described a variety of spiritual gifts (12:1-31a) and demonstrated that love is superior to all of them (12:31b—13:13). Here

Paul presented the proper application of spiritual gifts in the church. He identified prophecy as one of the most important spiritual gifts. In contrast, speaking in tongues is one of the least important gifts. Prophecy is superior to the gift of tongues because it builds up the church and communicates the gospel.

The Lesson Passage

1. Prophecy and Tongues Contrasted (14:1-11)

Paul encouraged the Corinthians to duplicate in their lives the love described in 1 Corinthians 13. Yet they should aspire to have certain spiritual gifts. Foremost of these was the gift of prophecy.

The popular definition of prophesy is "to foretell the future." While prophecy does contain a predictive element, it is not restricted to prediction. The Old Testament prophets were commissioned by God to stand before their world and cry out "Thus says the Lord!" In addition to conveying even distant future events, their task was to convey God's thought about a particular moment in history. The prophets sought to elicit faith in God from those who listened to their message. Their goal was to reconcile humanity with God.

All forms of the Greek term for prophecy were derived from a noun, which means "one who states aloud" or "makes known publicly," and always with a religious meaning. The prophet was one who spoke in the name of God. He occupied a mediatorial role between God and people who worshiped God. In the New Testament Era, a Christian prophet was a proclaimer of God's Word.[1] Prophecy was the declaration of God's will in a particular situation. The prophet spoke out on contemporary issues, declaring what God intended to do and what God desired people to do. The New Testament office of prophet was equal to the modern role of preacher.

Preaching is proclaiming God's message through personality to meet the needs of humanity.[2] Preaching, like prophecy in both Old and New Testaments, utilizes a person called by God to speak aloud a message from God. Delivering a message from God requires a self-disclosure of God to the prophet.

In the past God revealed Himself in various ways. His ultimate disclosure was the incarnation of Jesus Christ. The authority of Christian prophets resides in their fidelity in witnessing to God's revelation. Today, the only trustworthy record of that event is the Bible. Therefore, authoritative preaching is derived from the Bible. Preaching addresses the needs of those who listen. Preaching must seek to confront people with the living God through the proclamation of the Word of God.

Thus Paul exhorted his readers to desire the ability to communicate

God's revelation to the citizens of Corinth. The ability to share the truth should be desired more than any other spiritual gift. Witnessing to others about God's truth is the only method to alter the eternal destiny of other people (1 Cor. 1:18–2:5)!

A congregation does not benefit from one of its members speaking in tongues without an interpreter. Only those gifts that communicate an understandable message can help everyone. Paul put this premise in the form of a question with an obvious answer. The illustrations from life Paul referred to emphasized the importance of intelligibility. The flute or harp produce music by repeating recognizable sounds (v. 7). The bugle only communicates military orders when the soldiers can distinguish a known pattern of notes (v. 8). And while languages such as English and Hebrew may be valid forms of speech, they are gibberish to the one who speaks only Spanish or Greek (vv. 9-11).

2. Superiority of Prophecy (14:12-25)

The capacity to edify the believers in Christ's church and the ability to communicate God's truth are the two principles by which spiritual gifts are to be evaluated. Therefore, Paul proposed the superiority of prophecy in building up the church (14:12-19) and in proclaiming the truth of God (14:20-25)

Verse 12: *So also you, since you are zealous of spiritual gifts, seek to abound for the edification of the church.*

So also you is a repetition from verse 9. The phrase emphasizes the application that follows.

Paul did not wish to cool the zeal of the Corinthians. He wanted to redirect their zeal. Paul encouraged the use of the gift of prophecy because he realized that prophecy would edify **the church.** People who are genuinely spiritual will seek those gifts that can be used for the common good of the congregation. Paul hoped his readers might cease working to elevate themselves and cooperate so that the entire body might flourish. The importance of this idea may be seen in that this is the third time in the chapter that Paul mentioned the edification of the church. The effective use of *spiritual gifts* builds up the church.

Verses 13-17 contain practical instructions for the use of tongues and interpretation in the worship experience. Implicit in the discussion on speaking in tongues is the question of the usefulness of the gift for the edification of the body. The person gifted with tongues should petition God for the gift of interpretation also. Without interpretation the church cannot be edified by the gift of tongues. The usefulness of the spiritual gift of tongues for building up the church is dependent upon two critical factors. The message spoken in tongues must be translated to the congregation so they can understand what is said. And the congregation must have confidence that the translator's words are accurate.

Verse 13: *Therefore let one who speaks in a tongue pray that he may interpret.*

Therefore indicates that the command which follows is connected to the principle of edification established in verse 12. The *King James Version* has "an unknown tongue." Therefore, "speaking in the unknown tongue" is a common expression for this gift. The word *unknown,* however, is not in the Greek text, a fact denoted by the italicized print.

The technical term *glossolalia* often is used to denote the gift discussed in 1 Corinthians 12-14. This verse insinuates that *glossolalia* primarily was a form of prayer.

Today, many Christians speak in tongues. This practice involves uttering words and phrases which the speaker does not understand. The individual speaks rapidly, without thinking, and his or her words flow without hesitation.[3] Many believe this phenomena is the same as (or similar to) that described by Paul.

Charismatic Christians usually assert that the practice involves speaking a meaningful language. Some say the language may be an ancient language no longer spoken, or a language unfamiliar to the listeners, or an angelic language. Frequently, Acts 2:1-13; 10:46, and 19:6 are referred to as other references to point to the practice of speaking in tongues in the early church . The phenomena of Pentecost, however, seems different from the ecstatic speech at Corinth. At Pentecost the assembled crowd understood clearly the preaching of the apostles, each individual "hearing them speak in his own language" (Acts 2:6).

Verse 14: *For if I pray in a tongue, my spirit prays, but my mind is unfruitful.*

The exact meaning of **spirit** in this verse is uncertain. It probably does not refer to the Holy Spirit. English translations of the Bible have a lowercase "s," indicating that the word refers to a human spirit. *Spirit* may point to a person under the influence of the Holy Spirit. Whatever its precise sense, the contrast with **my mind** seems to imply a non-rational activity.

The word **mind** denotes understanding, thinking ability, or the capacity of intellectual perception. As part of the vocabulary of Greek philosophy and religion, it often was equivalent to reason. Here the sense is of an understanding that produces clear thoughts in intelligible words.[4] The point is that the Christian faith involves the whole person. Employment of one's intellectual ability does not lessen one's spirituality. Being spiritual and being intelligent are not conflicting ideas.

Verse 15: *What is the outcome then? I will pray with the spirit and I will pray with the mind also; I will sing with the spirit and I will sing with the mind also.*

Before speaking in a tongue, one should seek to discover how exercising this gift will benefit the hearers. The investigation should focus on both the individual user and the church body.

Both praying and singing are appropriate functions of public worship in the church. Paul rejected worship that was solely intellectual and so lacked emotion. Likewise, he spurned worship that was highly emotional but had little teaching of truth. Paul believed an individual should employ both intellect and fervor in public worship. The whole person must become involved in worshiping God.

Several years ago I was in Nicaragua, Central America. On Sunday morning I attended a local church. The music was wonderful. A recognizable hymn enabled me to sing a few words. But during the prayers and the sermon, my limited Spanish vocabulary deprived me of participation. The inability to use my mind deprived me of a complete worship experience. So too, when everyone in the Corinthian church spoke in tongues (as verse 16 points out) no one could understand the revelation. And no one could worship and give thanks.

Verse 16: *Otherwise if you bless in the spirit only, how will the one who fills the place of the ungifted say the "Amen" at your giving of thanks, since he does not know what you are saying?*

Next, Paul turned his attention to the other people worshiping in the assembly. What would be the impact on them of using the gift of tongues?

Who are **the ungifted?** Non-Christians is an obvious answer. Paul, however, made a distinction between "ungifted men" and "unbelievers" in verse 23. Here the ungifted have a **place** in the church. Therefore, Paul may have meant that they were inquirers. They had ceased to be outsiders to the congregation but had not yet made a commitment to Christianity. Or they may be a combination of inquirers and those church members who did not speak in tongues. Thus the term may apply to Christians or to non-Christians.

Amen is a transliteration of a Hebrew word. The Hebrew expresses the idea of a wish that God's revealed will may be done.[5] It was a way of expressing submission to the words and deeds of God. The word was used in response to a public prayer thereby making that prayer one's own. Saying **"Amen"** signifies agreement with what was said. If the hearer cannot understand the one speaking, such agreement is impossible! Therefore, the common language of those assembled for worship, Paul stated, was understandable words that communicates spiritual truth.

Verse 17: *For you are giving thanks well enough, but the other person is not edified.*

Paul acknowledged in principle that speaking in tongues was valid. While he insisted that nothing was wrong with praying in tongues, he contended its unintelligibility brought no edification to other believers in the church. Because of this lack of edification, the apostle preferred the gift of prophecy in the public assembly..

Verse 18: *I thank God, I speak in tongues more than you all;*

Paul acknowledged tongues as a spiritual gift. Therefore, he was grateful for having the ability to speak in tongues. And Paul employed his own experience as an object lesson to the Corinthians.

Paul pointed out that his objection to tongues was not due to his own lack of this spiritual gift. He insisted, **I speak in tongues more than you all.** This statement may have been inserted to prevent Paul's readers from objecting to his emphasis on using the gift of prophecy in the church rather than the gift of tongues. The Corinthian superspiritualists claimed that tongues was the evidence that one had received the Holy Spirit. Paul might not agree with their assertion, but he refused to allow his enemies to use it against him. And Paul sought common ground on which to assert his own point of view.

Verse 19: *however, in the church I desire to speak five words with my mind so that I may instruct others also, rather than ten thousand words in a tongue.*

Paul did not abuse the gift of tongues. He adopted the policy of never using tongues in public. He preferred **to speak five words** that were understood rather than ten thousand words that were not understood. Five was a typical small number. **Ten thousand** suggests infinite quantity. Paul considered instruction indispensable to building up of the church.

Verse 20: *Brethren, do not be children in your thinking; yet in evil be infants, but in your thinking be mature.*

Paul addressed his readers once more as **brethren.** The term was a reminder of his affection for them. It likewise is a reminder that differences of opinion concerning the spiritual gifts should not fracture one's relationship with fellow believers. Although Paul had a major disagreement with certain Corinthians, he continued to accept them as fellow Christians.

The grammar of this verse indicates an effort to stop action already in progress. The exhortation could be translated, "stop thinking like children." With one stroke of his pen, Paul challenged the basic assumption of the Corinthians. They believed that their pursuit of tongues revealed their spiritual maturity. Actually, it showed the opposite. Their selection of tongues as a sign that they were spiritual was not an evil resolution. It was a childish decision.

Mature Christians have the moral innocence of infants, and their **thinking** reflects the wisdom of experience. The Corinthians apparently claimed that the gift of tongues was an indication that a believer was spiritually mature. Paul contended that such an attitude was evidence of spiritual immaturity.

Verse 21: *In the Law it is written, "By men of strange tongues and by the lips of strangers I will speak to this people, and even so they will not listen to Me," says the Lord.*

The quotation is from Isaiah 28:11-12. Therefore, **the Law** refers to the entirety of the Old Testament and not specifically to the law of Moses. The original context of the quotation concerned Israel's failure to listen to the eighth century B.C. prophet, Isaiah. The nation stubbornly had refused to hear words spoken by the prophet in Hebrew, the language of the common people. Therefore, God was about to give them a new instructor, Assyria. The Assyrians spoke a language that was incomprehensible to the Israelites. Their conquest of God's people declared God's judgment of rebellion.

The application of the Old Testament passage to the situation in Corinth is not clear. Perhaps just as those who had refused to heed the prophet were punished by hearing speech that was not intelligible to them, so would it be in the Christian Era. Those who refused to believe would hear tongues instead of the clearly revealed will of God. Their inability to understand the speech was a declaration of divine judgment on their unbelief. It may be unnecessary to harmonize the original context of Isaiah 28:11-12 and its use here. Paul simply fortified his assertion that **tongues** was not a sign for believers by quoting Scripture. People cannot respond to God in faith and obedience if they cannot comprehend the meaning of the speech.

Verse 22: *So then tongues are for a sign, not to those who believe but to unbelievers; but prophecy is for a sign, not to unbelievers but to those who believe.*

A sign is an object, a person, or an event that identifies and validates something else. If **tongues** is a sign of God's presence, believers do not require it because God is present in their lives in the indwelling of the Holy Spirit. Although speaking in tongues is not *the* sign to show God's presence, it is a sign of God's judgment. Tongues is a sign in the sense that it leaves the unconverted in his or her fixed attitude of unbelief and rebellion toward God.

Prophecy (or preaching) is a sign for believers because of its value to the church. It delivers the message of God to His people in a manner in which they can comprehend its content. Then they can act obediently upon its meaning.

Verse 23: *Therefore if the whole church assembles together and all speak in tongues, and ungifted men or unbelievers enter, will they not say that you are mad?*

The use of **tongues** in public worship has a significant negative aspect. If people are present who are uneducated concerning this gift, they will conclude that the congregation was composed of deranged members. Likewise, non-Christians present would reach a similar conclusion and spurn Christianity because it did not make a favorable impression. It also is possible that this question may have been an implied warning that the ecstasy of the Corinthians, displayed by speaking in tongues, might be mistaken for pagan enthusiasm.

Verses 24-25: *But if all prophesy, and an unbeliever or an ungifted man enters, he is convicted by all, he is called to account by all; 25 the secrets of his heart are disclosed; and so he will fall on his face and worship God, declaring that God is certainly among you.*

In the same circumstances the effect of preaching is markedly different. Whereas speaking in tongues is perceived as a mark of madness, preaching leads to God. First, the unbeliever is convicted of his or her sin. Second, the unbeliever is called to account. The person becomes aware that individuals are responsible to God for their actions. Third, the final result from the use of prophecy is that the unbeliever is converted from pagan philosophies to the truth of Christianity.

3. Need for Order in Worship (14:26-40)

Paul's instructions to prohibit speaking in tongues whenever a interpreter is not present indicates that the spiritual gift of tongues (14:28) does not involve loss of self-control. Ecstasy that issues from an inability to control one's emotions or actions is not from God. Knowing that an interpretation will not be given, the person should remain quiet.

In unmistakable language Paul announced that in first-century churches women customarily remained silent in public worship. This practice may have been to safeguard the reputation of Christian worship in the eyes of the public. Paul did not wish to give people an opportunity to equate Christian women with pagan priestesses.

The Holy Spirit does not give spiritual gifts to divide believers. All spiritual gifts when used effectively build up the church and communicate the gospel to unbelievers. Differences of opinion exist within the Christian community about the continuing validity of tongues. Every individual is entitled to his or her position about the biblical intention. Billy Graham believes that when the gift of tongues is abused, it becomes divisive; when that happens, sin comes into the body of Christ.[6] Certainly, we can agree with his conclusion. The Holy Spirit does not divide Christ's body; He unites the body.

For Further Study

1. Read about prophecy and prophets in the *Holman Bible Dictionary,* pages 1141-1143 or in another Bible dictionary.
2. Can you improve your presentation of the gospel so that it is easier for individuals with no religious background to understand.

3. What is your spiritual gift? What do others say your spiritual gift is?

4. How are you using your gift to build up the church?

5. If you do not know your spiritual gift, what steps can you take to discover your gift?

1 *Dictionary of New Testament Theology,* 1976 ed., "Prophet" by Carl Heinz Peisker and Colin Brown, 3:74-75; *Theological Dictionary of the New Testament,* 1968 ed., "προφής" by Gerhard Friedrich and Helmut Krämer, 6:783-95,828-29.

2 John A. Broadus, *On the Preparation and Delivery of Sermons,* 4th ed., rev. by Vernon L. Stanfield (San Francisco: Harper & Row, 1979), 3.

3 Fisher Humphreys and Malcolm Tolbert, *Speaking in Tongues* (New Orleans, Louisiana: Insight Press, 1973), 1.

4 *Theological Dictionary of the New Testament,* 1967 ed., "νοέω" by Johannes Behm, 4:952-59.

5 *Theological Dictionary of the Old Testament,* 1974 ed., " אסן" by Alfred Jepsen, 1:320-21.

6 Billy Graham, *The Holy Spirit* (Waco, Texas: Word Books, 1978), 168.

August 10, 1997

Receiving the Gospel

Background Passage: 1 Corinthians 15:1-11
Focal Passage: 1 Corinthians 15:1-11

Introduction

The six year old autistic child ran into the street. In her mind the approaching truck presented no danger; but her mother instantly recognized its threat to her daughter. The mother immediately dashed into the street and quickly placed herself between her daughter and the truck. The driver was unable to stop in time. The mother was killed, but the daughter was saved. The husband said simply that His wife had died to save their daughter.[1]

When I read about this accident in the newspaper, it reminded me much of what Jesus has done for us. All of us have acted liked the little girl. We ignored God's guidance and commands. Such behavior put us in the direct path of divine justice, but we remained unconcerned about the danger! Then like the mother in the newspaper article, Jesus placed Himself on a cross between us and our destruction. The impact killed Him; but unlike the news story, our narrative has a happy ending. Three days later Jesus came forth from the grave. Death could not hold Him captive. He is alive today! We must remain firmly committed to such a wonderful Savior.

1 Corinthians 15:1-11
  1. Centrality of the Gospel (15:1-2)
  2. Explanation of the Gospel (15:3-8)
  3. Power of the Gospel (15:9-11)

The Background

Paul had followed his initial instructions about spiritual gifts with a discourse on the superiority of love. Then he encouraged his readers to develop their love and seek the gift of prophecy. He equated prophecy with preaching. In the present passage Paul set forth the content of that preaching, the gospel of the death and resurrection of Jesus Christ.

This is the climax of Paul's epistle to the Corinthians. He declared that the death and resurrection of Jesus is the most important truth of

Christianity. To Paul, any distortion of the gospel presented the most serious threat possible to the church.

Apparently, in Corinth some church members were denying a future resurrection. The problem was not that the Corinthians disbelieved the resurrection of Christ, but they had doubts about their own resurrection. Like the Sadducees, they may have maintained that death was the end of one's existence. There was no afterlife. Or they may have continued to embrace a Gentile perspective on death. The ancient Greeks believed that the soul was immortal, but they rejected the resurrection of the body. So Paul wrote this chapter to convince the believers at Corinth that because Christ rose from the dead they also would rise from the dead. His approach was to lay the foundation for Jesus' resurrection in the first 11 verses, a fact he acknowledged they believed (vv. 1,11).

Paul considered the Corinthian's point of view about their resurrection as far more dangerous than the divisions in the congregation (1 Cor. 1:10–4:21), the existence of sexual immorality (1 Cor. 5:1–40), or the arguments over Christian freedom (1 Cor. 8:1–11:1). Their erroneous view about the resurrection was even more significant than the abuse of spiritual gifts (12:1–14:40). The resurrection of the body was, and still is, vital to true Christianity. If Jesus Christ did not rise to live beyond the grave, those who believe on Him have no hope they will live past the grave. The truth that life on earth is a prelude to life to come for everyone who trusts Christ as Savior is a cornerstone of the Christian faith.

Paul reminded the Corinthians of their conversion experience. The Corinthian church had been the result of his own preaching ministry. Therefore, he recounted the content of his earlier ministry to them. His message embraced the fundamental truth of the Christian faith.

The Lesson Passage

1. Centrality of the Gospel (15:1-2)

The resurrection of Jesus Christ is the heart of the Christian faith and the foundation of the Christian belief in a general resurrection. Without the resurrection of Christ, the Christian faith is meaningless. If the resurrection of Jesus is not true, then Christianity takes its place alongside the world's religious speculations and philosophies.

Verse 1: *Now I make known to you, brethren, the gospel which I preached to you, which also you received, in which also you stand,*

In the New Testament the Greek verb translated here as **I preached** means "to bring good news," especially pertaining to military victories. Such news did not have to be factual. Because false stories of victory were spread in time of war to boost morale, the news often came to be treated with suspicion. On occasion the verb referred to political or private communication as in a letter. The theological application of the word develops this usage in relation to the message of salvation.[2]

The Christian application of the verb *preached* is not just preaching as a religious activity. It is proclamation with the full authority and power of God. The word **gospel** is the noun form of this verb. Together, they emphasize the wonderful news Paul disclosed in his speaking. And his good news was true. It was not propaganda. The gospel brought genuine victory to those who heard its words and received in faith its content.

The Corinthians had listened to Paul's preaching and accepted his proclamation as truth. Consequently, the church at Corinth was established through the people's decision to believe the gospel. The result of their acceptance was a continuing dependence upon the gospel's truthfulness.

Verse 2: *by which also you are saved, if you hold fast the word which I preached to you, unless you believed in vain.*

Previously, Paul had stated that the message of the cross was God's power for salvation (1 Cor. 1:18–2:5). He employed very precise language when he wrote to the church at Rome, "For I am not ashamed of the gospel, for it is the power of God for salvation to everyone who believes" (Rom. 1:16). When any individual hears the gospel and believes its message, the result is salvation.

If the Corinthians would **hold fast the word** Paul **preached** to them, their faith in the gospel of Christ declared their salvation. The grammatical construction of the Greek text indicated that this condition was a reality. The Corinthians *were* holding fast to the gospel; therefore, their salvation was a reality. If, however, they had rejected the gospel, their profession of faith was *in vain.*

Paul's statement, *if you hold fast,* does not mean that a believer can lose his or her salvation. Ultimately, God holds the believer; and as a result the believer continues in the faith. Abiding faith is evidence that God is holding the believer. One who professes faith in Christ and Christian living but rejects the gospel shows that his or her faith was never genuine. The professing believer's faith is, in Paul's words, *vain.*

Jesus taught about those who professed faith in Him but who had not trusted Him as their own personal Savior. He referred to gates and pathways that seemed to lead to the right way but only led to destruction (Matt. 7:13-14). He spoke about a house that had a weak foundation (Matt. 7:24-27) and of tares that looked like wheat but were not (Matt. 13:24-30,34-43). Jesus meant by these illustrations that a person can make a positive response to the gospel but not have genuine faith resulting in salvation. Many have faith that is *vain,* empty of the power He gives to **hold fast the word**.

The stress of Paul's words was on the content of that which is believed. One popular misconception claims that if people are sincere in their faith it really does not matter what or whom they believe. Paul refuted such logic. Faith in anything other than the Christ presented in Paul's proclamation of the gospel is *in vain.* Such faith cannot result in one's eternal salvation.

2. Explanation of the Gospel (15:3-8)

Paul proceeded to set forth the content of his preaching at Corinth. For Paul the gospel was the proclamation of the death and resurrection of Jesus Christ (15:3,4b). The evidence for Christ's death was His burial (15:4a). The proof of Christ's resurrection was His appearances to His followers (15:5-8).

Verse 3: *For I delivered to you as of first importance what I also received, that Christ died for our sins according to the Scriptures,*

The repeated use of *that* in 1 Corinthians 15:3-5 indicates that Paul was citing a Christian tradition. The clauses *I delivered* and *what I also received,* were terms for receiving and passing on this Christian tradition. The verbs implied that the gospel was imparted to Paul by other Christians. The apparent contradiction between Galatians 1:12 and 1 Corinthians 15:3 easily may be reconciled. The substance of the gospel (that the crucified Jesus of Nazareth is the risen Lord) was communicated to Paul from heaven while he journeyed to Damascus (Acts 9:3-6). However, the historical details of Jesus' earthly life and teachings were described to him by those who knew them.

Paul claimed that the message he received from other Christians and then proclaimed to the Corinthians was *of first importance.* The Greek clause may be translated "which is of the greatest importance." Nothing in the Christian faith can take priority over these truths.

The first part of the gospel is a declaration that *Christ died.* This identification of Jesus as the Christ marks Him as God's promised Messiah. The Christian gospel contradicted popular Jewish expectations for a warrior king to come and overthrow their Roman conquerors. But Christ's death is given significance by two qualifying phrases, *for our sins* and *according to the Scriptures.*

First, the death of Jesus was *for our sins.* The Greek preposition indicates that His dying was on our behalf. Thus it signifies both substitution and atonement. Christ died in our place (substitution) in order to remove our sins (atonement). Therefore, His death was God's solution to humanity's most basic problem—sin.

Second, Jesus' death took place in accordance with the teachings of the Hebrew Scriptures. Psalm 22:1-31 and Isaiah 52:13–53:12 are Old Testament passages that predicted Christ's death. The phrase *according to the Scriptures* seems to be deliberately general. It presupposed that the Corinthians were familiar with the Old Testament. Presumably, the phrase **according to the Scriptures** refers to all Scripture as a unity and indicates that the death of Christ was something foretold in the sacred writings. It proved, therefore, more than just the reality of His death. It showed that in keeping with Old Testament revelation about the Messiah, the purpose of Christ's death was for salvation.

Verse 4: *and that He was buried, and that He was raised on the third day according to the Scriptures,*

The death of Jesus was a literal, historical fact. Jesus' burial was visible proof of His death and, therefore, roots the gospel in history.

Paul's primary concern was to move beyond Christ's death to Christ's resurrection. The death of Christ was the consequence of our sin—not His sin. The resurrection was the divine act that declared the reality of Jesus' death on behalf of sinners. The tense of the Greek verb denotes that the resurrection was a past event and presently exists in a finished state. The passive voice of the verb indicates that the action of raising Jesus from the dead was by someone other than the one *raised.* Because only God has the power of life and death, resurrection was a divine activity. God raised Christ from the dead.

The specific **on the third day** reflects a literal conquest of death. According to Rabbinic tradition, the soul of the dead hovered near the corpse up to three days. After that, there was no hope of resuscitation.[3] Folklore's superstitious idea had been completed prior to the resurrection of Jesus. His return to life was more than a case of reviving someone from a coma or some other near-death experience.

Jesus' resurrection also was in harmony with the teachings of the ancient Hebrew sacred books. It was **according to the Scriptures.** Taken together with **on the third day,** the two descriptive phrases show that God had a predetermined plan. The resurrection was not a response to events over which God had lost control. Rather, it was the fulfillment of His own design for our salvation.

Verse 5: *and that He appeared to Cephas, then to the twelve.*

In verses 5-8 the list of witnesses to the resurrection is arranged in four groups. Each major section is marked by **He appeared** and each minor section by **then**.

The reality of Jesus' resurrection has substantiation by legal eyewitness evidence. Paul made no mention of the women who were the first to see the resurrected Lord. He probably omitted their testimony because it was not admissible as public evidence and therefore may have discredited his proof in the minds of first-century Gentile readers.[4] Paul wished to prove beyond a doubt, even to skeptics, that his preaching about Jesus being alive was true.

Cephas (Simon Peter) was the first apostolic witness to the resurrection (Luke 24:34). Therefore, he appeared first on Paul's list. The details of Jesus' appearance to Peter in Luke 24:34 are not recorded in the New Testament.

The twelve was an expression that designated the twelve apostles commissioned by Jesus (Luke 6:13-16). Presumably, this occasion was a reference to Christ's manifestation on Sunday evening (John 20:19-25). It also may include His appearance eight days later (John 20:26-29). On the first occasion of Jesus' appearance, Thomas was absent. Judas Iscariot already had hanged himself and so was not present at either incident (Matt. 27:3-5). Thus the term signified the group as a whole.

This is the only time Paul referred to **the twelve.** The apostle was indicating that his message was older than his own Christian experience. It was not Paul's invention.

Verse 6: *After that He appeared to more than five hundred brethren at one time, most of whom remain until now, but some have fallen asleep;*

This event cannot be equated with any incidence recorded in the gospels. Nor can its geographic location or time frame be determined. These were lay people who could testify from an unbiased viewpoint. A few of the 500 witnesses had died before Paul wrote this letter. Most, however, were still living at the time Paul wrote 1 Corinthians and could testify to the validity of the apostle's words.

Paul frequently referred to death by the analogy **some have fallen asleep.** He did not view death as the friend of the human race. Rather, it was the enemy of humanity, the horrible conclusion because of our sins. Sleep can be used as an euphemism for death only because Christ has conquered death. Death is a friend only to those who enjoy God's salvation. It remains the enemy of the unconverted until they, too, become believers in Jesus.

Verse 7: *then He appeared to James, then to all the apostles;*

James was the son of Joseph and Mary (Matt. 13:55; Mark 6:3). He grew up in the shadow of his elder brother Jesus. After Jesus began His earthly ministry, a wide spiritual distance separated Him from His family. James, along with his other brothers, sought to take Jesus into custody because they believed that He was mentally ill (Mark 3:21,31-35). They completely rejected Jesus' claim to be the Messiah (John 7:3-5).

James was gathered with those in the upper room prior to Pentecost (Acts 1:14). Therefore, he had been transformed dramatically after the crucifixion. Reasonably, the transformation Paul referred to in this verse was the result of this appearance by the risen Christ!

James immediately became an important member of the church in Jerusalem. Acts 12:17 seems to imply that James became the pastor of the church in that city. During the great conference called by the churches to settle the controversy resulting from Paul's first missionary journey, James was the dominating influence in the final decision. His influence extended throughout the Christian society. (See Gal. 2:12) At the time of Paul's last visit to Jerusalem, James was still the leading figure in that city. James also was the author of the New Testament epistle that bears his name.

The reference to **all the apostles** is unclear. Paul already had referred to the twelve by that terminology (v. 5). So he apparently was referring to another group here.

Verse 8: *and last of all, as it were to one untimely born, He appeared to me also.*

Paul listed the appearances in chronological order. He was the last person to see the risen Lord Jesus. With the addition of his own name, Paul's list of witnesses was complete. It did not include everyone who saw the resurrected Christ, but its scope was comprehensive enough to establish the resurrection as an irrefutable fact. Jesus had indeed been put to death, but He no longer was dead. Many people had seen Him alive!

This is the only occurrence in the New Testament of the Greek word rendered **one untimely born.** The word has a variety of meanings. It means "miscarriage," or "premature birth," or "untimely birth." Perhaps Paul's enemies used the term in a derogatory sense, implying that Paul was physically deformed in some way. Certainly, they were unimpressed by his presence (2 Cor. 10:10). Or perhaps Paul alluded to the sudden, unexpected nature of his conversion.

3. Power of the Gospel (15:9-11)

The death and resurrection of the Lord Jesus Christ is more than just a historical fact. Its proclamation can change the life of even its most bitter antagonist.

Verse 9: *For I am the least of the apostles, who not fit to be called an apostle, because I persecuted the church of God.*

Paul had once attempted to eradicate Christianity from the face of the earth. The first reference to Paul in the New Testament indicates that he was present at the stoning of Stephen (Acts 7:58). Those who participated in that mob action stripped their outer clothing, doubtless to lessen any restriction while throwing stones at Stephen. They placed their garments at the feet of Paul, then known as Saul, who was in full agreement with their deed.

Paul was a prominent Pharisee at the time of Stephen's martyrdom. He had received his training from Gamaliel, a most prestigious teacher in Judaism. Paul quickly became the leader of the Jewish persecution of Christianity. His involvement made him the worst enemy of the church. In his efforts to destroy the new sect, Paul's fury was without limit. He broke into the houses of suspected Christians, dragging both men and women away to prison (Acts 8:3). His efforts drove many believers out of Jerusalem. Thereafter, Paul sought either extradition papers or a letter of introduction and set out for Damascus to extend his persecution into that city. While on this wrathful mission to Damascus, Paul experienced the event that changed his life.[5] He encountered the risen Christ. Immediately, Paul went from persecutor to proclaimer, from one who worked to destroy the church to one who worked to build the church.

Verse 10: *But by the grace of God I am what I am, and His grace toward me did not prove vain; but I labored even more than all of them, yet not I, but the grace of God with me.*

Paul recognized that his hostility towards the church obliterated any personal merit. Christ's grace and Paul's subsequent salvation were undeserved in view of his sinful deeds. Full credit for the absolute reversal in the apostle's life rightfully belonged to God. Paul was changed from a ruthless persecutor to the zealous missionary **by the grace of God.** His new life was evidence that God's grace toward him was not futile.

Paul confessed that the gospel motivated him to work harder than most individuals. He acknowledged numerous successful efforts in preaching Christ. Paul did not, however, become haughty because of the mighty ways God had used him. He understood that these achievements were not the result of his own ability. Rather, they came as the effect of God's grace on his life experience. Therefore, even in his accomplishments God alone deserved the praise and honor.

Verse 11: *Whether then it was I or they, so we preach and so you believed.*

The gospel's ability to make the difference in one's life is not dependent upon the one who proclaims it. Paul noted that it did not matter **whether then it was I or they** who had preached to the Corinthians the message about Jesus. The content of the gospel message was the object of one's faith and hope. The Corinthians did not believe in Paul, but in the death, burial, resurrection, of Jesus Christ for their salvation. Paul exhorted the believers at Corinth to hold fast to the gospel in which they first had taken their stand.

Everyone who has been changed by the gospel is in one sense a witness of Jesus' resurrection. Therefore, we all have a responsibility to tell others about what happened to us. But the success of our effort does not depend upon individual eloquence or personal intelligence. Victory comes from the truth contained in our words. As long as we declare the gospel, the lives of people who hear and believe will continue to be changed by God's grace. Paul's life and ministry, committed as he was to proclaiming the good news about Jesus, is an example to all believers. We who know Christ also should testify to make Him known.

For Further Study

1. What are some things people think are more important than the gospel? How can you explain the gospel to people who feel this way? Write a letter in which you clarify the gospel of Jesus Christ.

2. Read "James: A Pillar of the Church," in the Fall 1988 issue of the *Biblical Illustrator.*

3. Read "The Kerygma" in the Winter 1993 issue of the *Biblical Illustrator.*

4. Read "Saul in Damascus" in the Spring 1993 issue of the *Biblical Illustrator.*

---

1 "Mother dies saving daughter from truck," *The Columbus Ledger-Enquirer,* Wednesday, August 30, 1995, p. C5.

2 *Theological Dictionary of the New Testament,* 1964 ed., "εὐαγγελίζομαι" by Gerhard Friedrich, 2:707; *Theological Dictionary of the Old Testament,* 1975 e.d., "בשר" by O. Schilling, 2:313-16; TWOT, 1980 ed.,"בשר" by John N. Oswalt, 1:135-36.

3 Raymond E. Brown, *The Gospel According to John* (i-xii): Introduction, Translation, and Notes, *The Anchor Bible,* ed. William Foxwell Albright and David Noel Freedman (Garden City, New York: Doubleday & Co., 1966), vol. 29, 424.

4 F. F. Bruce, 1 and 2 Corinthians, *New Century Bible Commentary* (Greenwood, South Carolina, Attic Press, 1971), 140.

5 D. Paul Smith, "Saul in Damascus," *Biblical Illustrator 19* (Spring 1993): 60.

August 17, 1997

Believing in Jesus' Resurrection

Background Passage: 1 Corinthians 15:12-34
Focal Passage: 1 Corinthians 15:12-20

Introduction

Few people who have read about Jesus dispute that He was a great figure in history. Moslems and some Jews agree that He was an important prophet. Even skeptics and agnostics do not dispute His impact on our world.

Christians acknowledge that He was a great preacher. His sermons were simple to understand yet profound in their implications (see Matt. 5:1—7:29). We cannot deny He changed the world and helped shape its present state. The strength of His preaching, however, is not the reason we follow Him. The reason is not His greatness as a historical ideologist. No, Jesus is more than a celebrated man. He is the living Lord. He is alive. His resurrection thrusts Him out of the past and confronts us with His life-changing presence today.

The resurrection of Jesus Christ is the central doctrine of the Christian faith. Apart from the resurrection the entire fabric of our religion unravels. If He is not alive, then our theological teachings and our Christian activities have no purpose. They do not result in any improvement in sinful humanity's destiny.

Jesus, however, did rise from the dead. Of this one reality we can be sure. Therefore, we Christians can live our lives with confidence that we too will experience a bodily resurrection.

1 Corinthians 15:12-34
1. The Heresy (15:12)
2. The Implications of the Heresy (15:13-19)
3. The Reality (15:20)
4. The Implications of the Reality (15:21-28)
5. Encouragement to Believe the Truth (15:29-34)

The Background

The Old Testament teaching on life after death was fragmentary. The majority of God's people during that era believed that the dead resided in a place known as Sheol. In Sheol no distinction was made between the righteous and the wicked (Job 21:23-26). After death an individual continued as a shade, a kind of replica of the once living person. The shade, they believed, resembled the person as the individual had existed in life. But all qualities of personality such as characterized the person upon the earth were absent.[1] There was no hope of escape from this gloomy existence (Job 14:7-22). Yet in this hopeless environment Job dared to declare that something more must come after the death of the body (Job 19:25-26).

The historical origins of a belief in the resurrection are obscure. By the close of the Old Testament Era, hope of resurrection was beginning to emerge (Isa. 26:19). During the period of the exile, a style of literature known as apocalyptic developed within the Jewish community. This literature employed symbolic language to tell of a divine intervention in history. While a few prophetic passages have apocalyptic features, Daniel is the only Old Testament book which is wholly apocalyptic.[2]

In apocalyptic writings a belief in a Messiah who would come and restore the glory of Israel emerged. In this style of literature, a stress on the restoration of a righteous Israel was combined with the idea that righteous individuals must share in this messianic kingdom. The idea necessitated a resurrection of the dead. By the first century A.D. the Pharisees and a great many ordinary people completely espoused the doctrine of a general resurrection of the dead. However, the teaching was not universal among the Jews. The Sadducees completely rejected the idea as being nonscriptural, but their opinion was in the minority.

For Paul the resurrection of Jesus was not merely the resurrection of God's Son. Paul had been a Pharisee, so he interpreted the reports of Jesus' resurrection from his own apocalyptic understanding of history. For the apostle Christ's resurrection signaled the beginning of the general resurrection of the dead. If Jesus was raised from the dead, then others surely must follow.

The good news about the resurrection of Jesus Christ shatters negative ideas about human worth. The resurrection declares that an individual matters to God. The essence of the gospel is set forth in 1 Corinthians 15:1-11. The intent of the gospel is that Jesus died and rose again for the person who receives the gospel.

The Lesson Passage

1. The Heresy (15:12)

Some Corinthians were saying that there was no resurrection of the dead. These individuals probably retained the Greek notion of the immortality of the soul. However, they found it difficult to conceive of the idea that a body which they believed to be evil would rise again. Paul realized that such logic struck at the very heart of the Christian faith.

Verse 12: *Now if Christ is preached, that He has been raised from the dead, how do some among you say that there is no resurrection of the dead?*

The verb **preached** always carries the basic meaning "to cry out loud," "to proclaim," "to declare," or "to announce." The verb is a derivative of the noun "herald." It was used of the herald announcing the winner of a contest. The term does not suggest the delivery of an accomplished and instructive speech in well-chosen words and a pleasant voice. The word **preached** is, rather, the declaration of an event.[3] Thus Paul used the verb to denote loud but clear vocal declaration of the historical resurrection of Jesus of Nazareth. Paul traveled to the city of Corinth, preached the resurrection, and as a result many of the Corinthians trusted Christ.

The announcement of Christ's resurrection is not supplementary to the proclamation of Christ. Rather, the resurrection of Christ is the essence of the Christian faith. Its proclamation is the public declaration of Christianity to the non-Christian world.[4]

It is strange that some of the believers heard Paul preach that Jesus was resurrected from the dead and believed the message. Yet they did not believe their own resurrection. How could they have accepted the one without the other?

In the previous lesson (August 10), it was pointed out how the Corinthians may have been influenced by the Greeks who believed the soul was immortal but rejected the resurrection of the body. This idea, called dualism and generally attributed to Plato, held that everything physical was evil and everything spiritual was good. So to the Greek mind the idea of a bodily resurrection was offensive. The afterlife, they thought, was an existence without being shackled to the confines of a physical body. Paul met this attitude when he preached on the Areopagus: "Now when they heard of the resurrection of the dead, some began to sneer" (Acts 17:32).

After Paul left the city of Corinth, perhaps this Greek idea of dualism infiltrated the church and caused doubts to occur in the believers' minds about their own resurrection. Those doubts Paul viewed as especially serious, and he sought to correct them in chapter 15.

The implications of that heresy could eventually lead to a denial that Christ arose, Paul thought. Logically, that was the case; for if they did not believe in a bodily resurrection how could Christ have been raised from the dead? And denying the resurrection of Christ struck at the cornerstone of Christianity. It was a dangerous situation that must not, Paul felt, continue without his forceful rebuttal. In response to the pressing need at Corinth, Paul set forth a rationale for the believers' resurrection.

2. The Implications of the Heresy (15:13-19)

Denial of the resurrection of the dead has numerous implications. In this passage Paul recorded several serious consequences of such heresy. Without a resurrection of the dead: (1) Jesus Christ remains dead (v. 13); (2) the gospel has no significance (v. 14a); (3) the Christian faith has no basis (v. 14b); (4) the apostles are liars whose descriptions of God and message of salvation are not true (v. 15); (5) personal faith in Christ is worthless (vv. 16-17a); (6) God has not forgiven people of their sins (v. 17b); (7) the Christian dead have vanished (v. 18); and (8) Christians are the world's biggest buffoons (v. 19). To dispute the resurrection is to deny the gospel and nullify one's own faith.

Verse 13: *But if there is no resurrection of the dead, not even Christ has been raised;*

You cannot believe in Christ and disbelieve in the resurrection of the dead. Faith in Him and faith in the resurrection are indivisible. Either resurrection can be a reality and thus **Christ** is alive, or there is no resurrection and so **Christ** is dead. If Christ is dead, then the Christ of the Christian faith is only a myth. He has no power to change the lives of people. He was a martyr who may inspire certain individuals to follow His teachings, but He is not a Savior who can transform their lives.

Verse 14: *and if Christ has not been raised, then our preaching is vain, your faith also is vain.*

If Christ has not been raised, then Paul's preaching was **vain. Vain** literally means "empty" or "without content." For example, the word pictured an empty cistern. **Vain** also was used figuratively of persons. In this case the word has the sense of describing one as "hollow" or "vain."

In this verse Paul indicated that if Christ was not raised from the dead the preaching and faith of Christians were without content and were ineffective.[5] If Christ were dead, the words of the gospel had no meaning. Therefore, they could never change one's life. For one to trust in such a false message, likewise, was pointless and powerless. It could never help an individual with real needs. Thus if Christ were not raised from the dead, Christianity was an empty, hollow religion.

Verse 15: *Moreover we are even found to be false witnesses of God, because we testified against God that He raised Christ, whom He did not raise, if in fact the dead are not raised.*

If there is no resurrection, the gospel is blasphemy. For if there is no resurrection, the gospel makes fraudulent claims about the activity of God. It claims that God **raised Christ** from the dead. But if there is no resurrection, God could not have raised Him from the dead. Then not only was Paul lying about God's deeds, the misrepresentation libeled God's character and nature. Paul's preaching assumed God's power was unlimited. It also presumed that His love for people had caused Him to act. However, *if in fact the dead are not raised,* then either God was too weak to raise the dead or His love for humanity was insufficient to motivate His action. Either way, God's power and love proclaimed by believers is not true.

Verse 16: *For if the dead are not raised, not even Christ has been raised;*

Verse 16 repeats verse 13. If there is no resurrection, the crucifixion terminated the life and ministry of Jesus. A person's faith in Jesus' resurrection does not rest upon a theory but upon the historical fact of His resurrection. Just as the burial of Jesus (15:4) is historical proof of His death, the appearances of Jesus (15:5-8) are historical proofs that His resurrection occurred. The resurrection declares that Jesus' death for our sins was effective.

Verse 17: *and if Christ has not been raised, your faith is worthless; you are still in your sins.*

If Jesus is dead, then faith in Him is **worthless. Worthless** is not wholly a synonym for "in vain." Whereas "in vain" means something is useless because it is without content, **worthless** has the implication that it is useless because it is against the norm, unexpected, and offending what ought to be. The former means worthless because of a lack of content. The latter means worthless because it is deceptive.[6]

If Jesus is dead, then death (the outcome of human sin) overcame Him; and sin defeated Christ. Thus without the resurrection of Christ, Christians remain in a state of unforgiven sin. Without the resurrection of Christ, redemption from sin cannot be a reality for sinners! Without the resurrection of Christ, divine forgiveness is an illusion; it does not exist. Christians are no different from the worst infidel and will share his or her eternal destiny. Without the resurrection the believer is no better off than the unbeliever.

Verses 18: *Then those also who have fallen asleep in Christ have perished.*

Paul referred to physical death for Christians as sleep. Dying is like lying down at night for a period of rest that includes the expectation of awaking the following morning and resuming activity. Death is something to anticipate with cheer and not to be feared.

The metaphor implies that the Christian who dies, in reality, remains alive. Life after death is true because salvation is equated to receiving eternal life (John 3:16). If the gift of life is eternal, death becomes an impossibility. But the reality of death as sleep only exists for the individual who has heard the gospel and has faith in the risen Christ. For those who reject the gospel, death is an eternal horror. Rejecting the gospel is an event that brings terror rather than rest.

Verse 19: *If we have hoped in Christ in this life only, we are of all men most to be pitied.*

Christian hope is beyond anything this life can promise. If that hope is not a reality, then believers are to be pitied. *Most to be pitied* is the comparative degree of pitiable, meaning that believers should be the object of people's sympathy and compassion because they have hoped in resurrection and resurrection will not be realized.

I sometimes hear Christians say they would be a Christian even if there were no heaven. Such a declaration reflects the joy of life lived in harmony with God. Without the resurrection, however, such harmony would be impossible. Thus, the peace that such statements presume would not exist. Life would be quite different if there was no heaven.

If there is no resurrection, Christians are the object of the greatest hoax in history. Therefore, intelligent people should consider them fools and take pity on them.[7]

3. The Reality (15:20)

Paul's numerous results from denying the resurrection are only hypothetical. Christ, in fact, has been raised from the dead.

Verse 20: *But now Christ has been raised from the dead, the first fruits of those who are asleep.*

This is an emphatic statement of the truth. **Christ has been raised from the dead.** His resurrection is the **first fruits** of the general resurrection of the righteous dead. Again, the metaphor of sleep indicates that Paul was referring to Christians in this passage.

The **first fruits** were the first gathering in a harvest. They assured the farmer that his crop was a success. More harvest would be gathered as well. This analogy implies more than the fact that Christ's resurrection was the first of its kind; it insists that more resurrections (of believers) will follow! Christ's resurrection is a prelude to believers' resurrection. He is alive; believers will live after death too!

4. The Implications of the Reality (15:21-28)

Verses 21 and 22 are parallel statements. Adam's sin brought death to all, but Christ's death and resurrection brings life to all who believe in Him. Paul interpreted man's original sin as damaging all human existence. Since Adam disobeyed God (Gen. 3:1-7), something has been fundamentally wrong with humanity. Human depravity not only makes sin possible but makes sin certain as the world's evil history shows. Sin always results in death. Thus all human beings die. The cemeteries of the world bear conspicuous testimony to this universal and tragic reality.

Whereas every mortal shares in the consequence of Adam's deed, the "all" who will "be made alive" is limited to those who are "in Christ" (v. 22). An individual is "in Christ" through faith and by choice. Therefore, only Christians enjoy the resurrection. Those not in Christ will be resurrected only to incur eternal judgment. This is not life in the Christian sense but an eternal existence of torment and retribution. In verses 21-22 Paul's interest was on the effect of the gospel his readers had accepted, not a essay about heaven and hell. So he limited his focus to the resurrection of believers.

There are two states, the living and the dead. No interim condition exists between the two. Christ's reign as Lord is fact, but His authority is still disputed. The last enemy to be subjected to Him will be death. The resurrection is the abolition of death; therefore, after the resurrection only life will remain.

God has prescribed a specific order for those events that will usher in the eternal reign of Christ (15:23). The resurrection of Christ was the first. The resurrection of Christians will be next. Some biblical scholars insist that "the end" should be rendered "the rest." If this is the correct interpretation, Paul was indicating that non-Christians would be raised last. Regardless, after the dead are raised the consummation of the present age will come. All forces that work against God will cease (15:24). The last enemy to be terminated is death (15:26). After the termination of death, nothing will obscure the reality that Jesus Christ is Lord. Everyone will acknowledge His reign (Phil. 2:9-11). Once He is fully revealed as Lord, the Son will acknowledge His subjection to the Father (15:28).

5. Encouragement to Believe the Truth (15:29-34)

Paul set forth the life of a believer as an argument for the resurrection of the dead. The behavior of Christians cannot be explained if the resurrection is not a fact. Paul directed the Corinthians to examine their actions and ask, "Why do we do this?" The only explanation was the resurrection of Jesus and their belief in His resurrection.

1 Corinthians 15:29 presents a major difficulty. What does "baptized for the dead" mean? Many possible interpretations have been proposed. First, it may mean that people were being saved and baptized because of the Christian witness and the exemplary lives of those who had died. Second, Paul may have referred to some abnormal baptism known only to the Corinthians, which would be meaningless without a belief in the resurrection. Third, Paul may have referred to a possible existing proxy baptism, which he used as an argument for the resurrection without giving approval to the practice. Fourth, more likely the statement means that people were being baptized in the sense of replacing those Christians who had died. New converts entered the faith as older members died. But the continuation of the church would be pointless if there were no resurrection of the dead. Whatever its meaning, the practice of baptizing for the dead showed the reality of the resurrection by the

Corinthian believers, even if they did not perceive that reality as they baptized.

Christians frequently faced danger in the first century. Paul recounted an incident in his own experience as an illustration (15:32). It occurred while he was in Ephesus. We cannot identify the incident with any specific episode described elsewhere in the New Testament. "Wild beasts" is probably a metaphor. The reason is that Roman law prohibited a Roman citizen, such as Paul, to fight wild animals as punishment. Besides, in such cases the victim was killed by the beast. Paul was alive.

"I die daily" means that Paul considered himself dead to a personal agenda so that he might be free to serve Christ better. He placed the welfare of the Christian believers' faith above his own personal need. Christianity changes the lifestyle of believers. Christians often give up material things and physical pleasures for the spiritual growth of others. Regularly, they encounter the abuse of non-Christians. Most often abuse is mental. However, sometimes Christians, like Paul, even suffer physically because of their convictions about the gospel.

If there is no resurrection, then the deprivation Christians sometimes endure is illogical. During the Old Testament Era, the prophet Isaiah announced God's judgment on Jerusalem. Rather than repent, the ancient citizens of Judah celebrated. They chose the philosophy, "Let us eat and drink, for tomorrow we die" (Isa. 22:13). If there is no resurrection, Christians would be wise to follow their example!

"Bad company corrupts good morals" was quoted from a Greek poet. The statement first appeared in a play by Menander. Menander was an Athenian dramatist whom ancient critics considered the supreme poet of Greek New Comedy. He wrote more than 100 plays, but he had limited success in his lifetime. His works later were adapted by the Roman writers, Plautus and Terence.[8] Paul used the quotation to warn his readers to be careful with whom they associated.

"Become sober-minded" literally means to awake from a drunken stupor. Here the expression has the sense to come back to one's senses, to think clearly and wisely again.

Paul concluded that the reason some of the Corinthians doubted the resurrection was because they did not know God! They had never experienced a relationship with Him based on personal trust. Therefore, they had no knowledge of Him.

The failure of the Christians in Corinth to recognize the true reason for their denial of the resurrection was a disgrace. Genuine believers needed to repent for listening to such foolishness. Their life was to be established firmly on the resurrection of the Lord Jesus Christ. Without the fundamental foundation of the risen Christ, Christianity crumbles before the onslaught of the world. In the presence of the risen Lord, however, Christians find the true motivation for living.

For Further Study

1. Read "The Reality of Jesus' Resurrection" in the Winter 1994 issue of the *Biblical Illustrator.*
2. Read about resurrection in the *Holman Bible Dictionary,* pages 1178-1179, or in another Bible dictionary.

---

1 D. S. Russell, *The Method & Message of Jewish Apocalyptic: 200BC-100AD,* Old *Testament Library,* ed. G. Ernest Wright, John Bright, James Barr, and Peter Ackroyd (Philadelphia, Pennsylvania: Westminster Press, 1964), 354.

2 *Holman Bible Dictionary,* 1991 ed., "Apocalyptic" by George Beasley-Murray, 68.

3 *Theological Dictionary of the New Testament,* 1965 ed., "κῆρυξ" by Gerhard Friedrich, 3:697-703.

4 C. H. Dodd, *Apostolic Preaching and Its Development* (Grand Rapids: Baker Book House, 1936), 7.

5 *Theological Dictionary of the New Testament,* 1965 ed., "κένόσ" by Albrecht Oepke, 3:659-60.

6 *Theological Dictionary of the New Testament,* 1967 ed., "μάταιοσ" by O. Bauerfeind, 4:519.

7 *Theological Dictionary of the New Testament,* 1964 ed., s.v. "ἔλεοσ" by Rudolf Bultmann, 2:478.

8 *Encyclopedia Britannica Micropaedia,* 1978 ed., "Menander," 6:781.

August 24, 1997

Believing in Our Resurrection

Background Passage: 1 Corinthians 15:35-57
Focal Passages: 1 Corinthians 15:35-38,50-57

Introduction

Several years ago I had the privilege to talk with author and evangelist Vance Havner. Not long before our conversation, Dr. Havner's wife, Sara, died. During the conversation, he shared about the death of his beloved wife. He told about the many friends who remarked how sorry they were to hear he had lost her. Then with fire in his eyes, Dr. Havner looked squarely into my face and said, "I didn't lose her. I know exactly where she is!" I have often thought about his words. Sara Havner was a Christian. Therefore, the Bible says she is present with the Lord (2 Cor. 5:8). Too many times Christians allow human opinion and personal experience to become more real to them than God's promise of life.

God promised that those who believe in the Lord Jesus Christ will have eternal life. Yet sometimes the realities of funeral services, deceased family members, and acres of tombstones distract our attention from this wonderful hope. But Christians, even though they are surrounded by death, will be resurrected; and they will receive new bodies that will last forever. God's promise of bodily resurrection guarantees the Christian's life beyond this world.

People need to know the truth. They are searching for immortality but are looking in the wrong place. The eastern theory of reincarnation has gained widespread devotees. But when people die, they do not return to earth in another life. Only the Christian doctrine of the resurrection offers genuine hope to people.

1 Corinthians 15:35-57
    1. The Question (15:35)
    2. The Answer (15:36-44)
    3. The First Adam and the Last Adam (15:45-49)
    4. The Reason (15:50)
    5. The Mystery (15:51-54)
    6. The Victory (15:55-57)

The Background

The Corinthians were having trouble believing in their own resurrection. How could they die and then come back to life? Their question was not so much inquisitive as it was a denial of bodily resurrection.

Paul provided his readers with some analogies for understanding the resurrection. He used illustrations from botany, zoology, and astronomy. The problem he addressed concerned the understanding of the resurrection body. Therefore, he contrasted a seed and its plant (15:37); a human body and an animal (15:39); and the sun, moon, and stars to earthly bodies (15:40-41). Then he explained that there also is a contrast between the physical body that dies and the resurrection body that is raised. Because flesh and blood cannot inherit the kingdom of God, God promises Christians a new body that will last forever (15:42-49).

Verses 50 through 58 are a conclusion and exhortation. When Christians have received their resurrected glory, then the promise of victory over sin and death will be complete and final!

The Lesson Passage

1. The Question (15:35)

Questions about the resurrection are natural. People still wonder about the nature of the resurrected body.

Verse 35: *But someone will say, "How are the dead raised? And with what kind of body do they come?"*

Within Judaism certain sects, such as the Pharisees, debated the nature of the resurrection body. They developed a tightly formulated doctrine on the resurrection. They taught that the resurrection body was exactly like the one that died. Others, such as the Sadducees, repudiated any expectation that the dead would be raised. Their strictly literal interpretation of the law and rejection of all other Scripture and traditions meant that they denied any hope for an afterlife. So instead of putting their trust in any expectation of resurrection after death, the Sadducees placed their hope for the future in a better Israel. The Greeks believed in the soul's immortality, but not in a resurrection of the physical body. They believed the body was evil. Therefore, to escape evil one had to depart the physical body. In such a diverse and skeptical environment, questions such as *"How are the dead raised?"* and *"And with what kind of body do they come?"* could be expected by the Corinthian believers.

2. The Answer (15:36-44)

Paul's illustrations in these verses show that both continuity and discontinuity exist in the resurrection body. The resurrected body is not the same body that was placed in the grave. Nor is it unrelated to that body.

Verse 36: *You fool! That which you sow does not come to life unless it dies;*

You fool was a strong expression of reproach. Paul was thinking that if the Corinthians would only open their eyes they might understand that nature points to resurrection. In the second part of the verse, Paul was not emphasizing the continuity of life nearly as much as he was stressing the difference between physical life and life after the resurrection of the body. He did not write about germination as if he were a botanist. Rather, Paul described what could be observed by a nonfarmer. **Dies** was symbolic of ceasing to exist. Paul pointed out that a farmer buried the seed. Then a plant, not the seed, came forth from the soil. The seed ceased to exist.

Verse 37: *and that which you sow, you do not sow the body which is to be, but a bare grain, perhaps of wheat or of something else.*

Continuing with his agriculture metaphor, Paul showed that it was obvious to expect some change at death. For a farmer to sow a mature wheat plant would be absurd. He plants only a tiny seed. There is a vast difference between the seed that was planted beneath the ground and the plant that grows above the ground. That difference is true of every crop. Like the vegetation and its seed, there are differences between the human body that is buried and the body that is raised. Some of these differences were demonstrated in part by Christ during His appearances after the resurrection. He was able to appear and vanish instantly (Luke 24:31; John 20:19,26) and was not restrained by the natural laws of time and space.

Verse 38: *But God gives it a body just as He wished, and to each of the seeds a body of its own.*

God gives the sown seed its body according to His own desire. Corn seeds produce corn plants, not tomato plants. Thus some continuity exists between physical life and resurrection life.

Continuity also can be illustrated from the appearances of the resurrected Christ. Those who encountered the risen Lord were able to identify Him as the same Jesus who was crucified. Because of the disciples' unbelief, this identity sometimes was slow in coming. Nonetheless, in every case their realization that the One speaking was Christ eventually overwhelmed all uncertainty. These appearances reveal that the risen Christ had some type of physical body that retained the scars from His crucifixion (Luke 24:39; John 20:20,27). In addition, Jesus was able to eat physical food (Luke 24:41-43), showing that He retained certain characteristics of His earthly life.

People have far more questions about the nature of the resurrection body than the Bible provides answers for. One cannot make a precise comparison from the appearances of the risen Christ. He is divine. Thus some of His activity may issue more from His divine nature than from the characteristics of His raised body. Nonetheless, both the gospel narratives and Paul's words here insist that there is both continuity and differences between the earthly body and the resurrection body.

Scholars differ on the interpretation of "heavenly bodies" (15:40). Some insist they are the stars, the moon, the sun, or other kinds of heavenly objects. However, others argue that they are celestial beings such as angels. Still others propose that heavenly bodies refers to the stars being perceived as living creatures. Regardless of who might be correct, the understanding of the verse remains the same. A vast difference exists between earthly bodies and stars, or human bodies and angelic bodies, or people and stars described as living creatures.

Whatever the meaning of the phrase "heavenly bodies" might be, Paul noted that in the universe an infinite variety of celestial bodies exist. He named the sun, the moon, and the stars. The sun is an incandescent body of gases, and produces light, heat, and energy for the entire solar system. The sun's diameter is about 865,000 miles. The moon is a smaller body whose surface is composed of rock and dust. Its illumination at night is a reflection of the sun's light. The moon's diameter is only about 2,160 miles. The stars vary in size and brightness. Although some are much larger than the sun, the distance between them and the earth give them the image of being smaller. Each of these elements of our universe has its unique place.

Finally, Paul contrasted the human corpse that is buried with the body that is resurrected. The corpse is "perishable" (15:42). From birth the human body goes through the process of aging. By studying demographics, one's life expectancy can be projected at birth. For example, baby boys born in the United States during 1972 were projected on the average to live to an age of 67 years. Baby girls were expected to live 75 years.[1] One point from such projections cannot be lost—life has a limitation. The human body cannot function indefinitely. In contrast, the new body is "imperishable." It has no temporal limitations but has been designed by God to never die again.

The earthly body is marked by **dishonor** and **weakness** (15:43). The Greek term for **dishonor** does not so much imply disgrace as it denotes the absence of "glory."[2] The word sometimes described the loss of the rights of citizenship. So Paul may have suggested that a corpse has no rights. And certainly he knew a decaying body buried in the grave possessed no glory or honor. The physical body, however, does have basis for esteem. Its resurrection will change its status. The body's transformation by the power of God provides it with real honor and prestige. The body's perfection after its resurrection is cause to give glory to God.

In life the human body is relatively feeble. In death it is completely powerless. The power of God, however, which already has raised Jesus from the dead, will empower the resurrected body.

In verse 44 Paul did not imply that the body after the resurrection will be a spirit as opposed to flesh and bone. In reference to His own body, Jesus condemned this conclusion (Luke 24:39). Rather, these terms must be understood in light of the usefulness of the body. The "natural body" is suitable for the present age, but the "spiritual body" is for the age to come. A "spiritual body" is one made alive by the power of the Holy Spirit. The process of salvation is complete, and this body is fit to be in the presence of God. The reality of this spiritual body is as certain as one's present existence.

3. The First Adam and the Last Adam (15:45-49)

Humanity gets its physical life from Adam. Human existence can be traced through the process of procreation back to Adam and Eve. Adam was made from the dirt of the earth. God breathed life into his existence (Gen. 2:7).

From Christ we get our spiritual life. Christ is the last Adam. He did not become a "living soul" but a "life-giving spirit." Even though the life Christians have comes from Christ, their present earthly life is limited by time. At death Christians depart the physical life in order to fully participate in the spiritual life.

4. The Reason (15:50)

Paul brought his discussion to a dramatic climax. His language was the plainest possible. He desired his readers to understand that the promised resurrection body was necessary.

Verse 50: *Now I say this, brethren, that flesh and blood cannot inherit the kingdom of God; nor does the perishable inherit the imperishable.*

Paul addressed Christians; he called them **brethren.** First-century society was male oriented, and the language reflected that environment. Thus, both sexes are included in the terminology. Paul's **now I say this** is akin to Jesus' "Verily, verily." Both expressions denoted something of extreme importance. Paul's words have the sense of, "Listen carefully. What I am about to say is very important."

Flesh and blood symbolize physical life in the present age. Physical life is subject to decay and dissolution. The present human condition has been corrupted by sin. Death is the penalty for sin (Gen. 3:19), so fallen humanity cannot belong to God's perfect kingdom. Furthermore, the kingdom of God is a permanent order. Consequently, that which does not possess the quality of absolute permanence cannot become a part of that kingdom. A transformation must take place first. That transformation occurs at death.

The phrase **the kingdom of God** denotes that time when the sovereignty of God will be undisputed and His reign no longer is challenged. Satan, sin, and their followers will be banished. The dominion of God as King will be disclosed completely. Everything will be in harmony with His rule.

5. The Mystery (15:51-54)

Verses 51 through 57 form the conclusion to Paul's discourse on the resurrection. Having informed the Corinthians about the consequences of death, there was another truth Paul addressed. Christ had promised to return to earth again. Thus someone might ask "What happens to those who have not died when Christ returns?" Therefore, Paul shifted from the subject of death and resurrection to the second coming of Christ. His words state a crescendo of results that come from the resurrection and will become evident at the Lord's return. Mortal existence will be transformed into immortality. Death, sin, and the law will be abolished. Christ's victory will be absolute! And Christians shall share forever in this victory Christ won!

Verse 51: *Behold, I tell you a mystery; we will not all sleep, but we will all be changed,*

The word **mystery** points to an idea beyond human comprehension without God's revelation of its meaning. Elsewhere, Paul used the term to describe ideas that already had been realized and the previously hidden meaning made known. For instance, in Ephesians 3:1-21 the inclusion of the Gentiles in God's kingdom is labeled a mystery. In verse 51, however, the term marks an event in the future. Not everyone will die. Some will still be living when Christ returns. But transformation will be necessary for them as well as those who have died in Christ.

Verse 52: *in a moment, in the twinkling of an eye, at the last trumpet; for the trumpet will sound, and the dead will be raised imperishable, and we will be changed.*

Expressions such as **in a moment** and **in the twinkling of an eye** convey the speed of the transformation of those who are alive when the Lord returns. The change will be too fast to measure. The use of **we** may indicate that Paul believed he would still be living when Christ returns. Christians should anticipate His second coming.

Paul did not provide all the details that will surround the second coming. He noted that **the trumpet will sound.** This will be followed by the resurrection of the dead and the transformation of the living. According to 1 Thessalonians 4:13-18, the blowing of the trumpet of God will be accompanied by Christ descending from heaven with a shout and the cry of the archangel. In that passage Paul emphasized that the transformation of the living will not precede the resurrection of the dead. Both will meet the Lord in the air. The essence of both passages is that Christians should never despair. Death holds no power over them. The resurrection will bring victory over death.

Verse 53: *For this perishable must put on the imperishable, and this mortal must put on immortality.*

Perishable may designate those who already had died. The dead in Christ must be raised. Decay and destruction for believers no longer will be possible after the resurrection. **Mortal** may designate the living in that they have the potential to die. Death, however, no longer will exist after the resurrection. Another interpretation of these two words *(perishable* and *mortal)* is that they may be synonyms, meaning that the two words refer to the human body's certainty of death. However one understands these two terms, the important point Paul made is the necessity of bodily change when Christ returns.

Verse 54: *But when this perishable will have put on the imperishable, and this mortal will have put on immortality, then will come about the saying that is written, "Death is swallowed up in victory.*

Paul repeated the message of the previous verse; only he changed the tense of the verbs from future tense to past tense. This literary style underscored the certainty of God's promise of resurrection. The apostle supported this certainty by alluding to Isaiah 25:8. He did not quote the verse from either the Hebrew text or the Greek translation of the Hebrew (the Septuagint). Rather, he paraphrased the verse by placing the language of the predictive prophecy in a statement of completed fact. The resurrection of the saints fulfills that which Isaiah foretold.

6. The Victory (15:55-57)

Paul's final remarks on the resurrection are powerful words of praise and gratitude. He scoffed in the face of sin and death. His scorn, however, was not the folly of reckless boasting. It was derived from his firm conviction in the reality and results of Christ's resurrection.

Verse 55: *"O death, where is your victory? O death, where is your sting?"*

In this verse Paul taunts death. Turning to Hosea 13:14 in its original context, the passage was an invitation for death to come and destroy the Northern Kingdom of Israel because of the Israelites stubborn refusal to repent of their sins. Paul applied the verse to show that the role death once played no longer is true for believers. The death of Jesus made atonement for sin, and His resurrection insured that the accomplished redemption is true. Like a bee that stings, leaving its stinger in the victim, death left its sting in Christ when He died on the cross. Christ took death's sting so we would not have to bear it. Consequently, death is no longer a destroyer to the believer. Because of Christ, death brings the believer bodily resurrection, into God's presence, and to immortality.

Again, Paul paraphrased the Old Testament passage. Here he changed the term "thorns" to *victory.* The change rendered both the Isaiah and Hosea references with the terms "death" and "victory." The verbal form of the Greek word for victory expresses visible superiority in a rivalry among people. The corresponding noun represents victory, or the power that confers victory. The feminine form, *Nike,* was the name of the Greek goddess who was a symbol of personal superiority.[3] Paul challenged death to disclose its superiority over humanity. He dared death to reveal its ability to hurt God's people. Because of the resurrection, death's inferiority and powerlessness has been overcome.

Verse 56: *The sting of death is sin, and the power of sin is the law;*

The sting of death is its ability to hurt people. Only because of sin can death inflict its fatal blow. Therefore, sin is the sting of death because death gains sway over individuals through sin (Rom. 5:12; 6:23; 7:8-11). However, because sin's guilt has been removed from the believer, death only ends the earthly life and begins the heavenly life. Death is still an experience for the believer, of course, but its sting, sin, *is* gone. Even though Christians sin, the sins they commit are covered by the blood of Christ; consequently, sin's effect is not permanently fatal. Sin's sting is removed because of Christ's victory over death. The sting is disarmed, destroyed, and declawed!

The revealed **law** of God refers to His standards. When a person breaks God's standard, the law reveals the person's sin and makes the sinner conscious of sin. It intensifies sin in the life of an individual (Rom. 3:20; 4:15; 7:8). Consequently, people die because they choose to break God's laws. Even those who do not know God's written law violate His law when they act against their conscience (Rom. 2:14-15).

Verse 57: *but thanks be to God, who gives us the victory through our Lord Jesus Christ.*

Paul ends with a statement of thanksgiving. Christians should give thanks **to God** because of the resurrection. Only the grace of God can liberate the sinner from the bondage of sin and death. The power of God's liberation is the resurrection of Jesus Christ.

This is the third time Paul used the word *victory* in four verses. First he noted that death was swallowed up by victory. Then he asked death what had become of its victory. Finally, he declared that victory has been given to the Christians! The victory of death over humanity demonstrates sin's grave consequence over humanity. The victory of Jesus over death, however, demonstrates His superiority over sin's consequences. And God's grace elevates the Christian to a position of superiority over both sin and death! Neither have power over us. This ultimate reality should challenge us to live life totally committed to God.

For Further Study

1. Compare and contrast Paul's statements on the second coming of Christ in 1 Corinthians 15:51-58 with 1 Thessalonians 4:13-18.

2. Read about the second coming in the *Holman Bible Dictionary*, pages 1240-1241, or in another Bible Dictionary.

3. What are some assurances Paul's words in 1 Corinthians 15:53-54 provide to adults who have lost family and friends to death or who might be facing their own death?

---

1 Carroll B. Freeman, *The Senior Adult Years* (Nashville: Broadman Press, 1979), 32.

2 Bruce, 1 and 2 Corinthians, *NCB,* 152.

3 *Dictionary of New Testament Theology,* 1976 ed., "Fight" by Walther Günther, 1:650.

August 31, 1997

Giving Ourselves and Our Resources

Background Passage: 1 Corinthians 15:58–16:24
Focal Passage: 1 Corinthians 15:58–16:9

Introduction

Have you ever thought about what it takes to operate your church? Money, for instance, is essential. Utility companies do not donate electricity, gas, water, and other services. The staff and other employees must be paid. Literature must be purchased. Foreign and home missionaries need our prayers and financial backing. (We agreed to support them when we sent them to the mission field.) Paper, ink, office equipment, and cleaning supplies are not free. These are but a few of the items listed in your church budget.

Money, however, is only one requirement. Your church needs countless hours of volunteer work by its members. People must donate their time to serve on the various committees, lead Bible studies, provide child care for pre-school age children, sing in the choir, and a host of other projects.

In today's world the church competes with numerous other organizations and activities for resources and people. Therefore, it is vital for Christians to remain loyal to their Lord and to the ministries of their church. Their commitment should motivate them to give of themselves and their resources to the work of the Lord. God has promised that the believers' efforts will not fail.

1 Corinthians 15:58–16:24
1. Giving Ourselves (15:58)
2. Giving Our Resources (16:1-4)
3. Helping Others Serve (16:5-18)
4. Conclusion (16:19-24)

The Background

Paul concluded his letter with a challenge to the Corinthian Christians to be unwavering in the faith (15:58). He urged them to give themselves and their resources to the service of Christ. One specific application of this exhortation concerned their financial assets. Paul gave them instructions about collecting a weekly offering for the poor Christians in Jerusalem (16:1-4). Because he was planning to visit Corinth later in the year, Paul desired the Corinthians to support him in his next mission venture (16:5-9). He urged the Corinthians to treat hospitably, Timothy, whom Paul was sending to the church at Corinth (16:10-12). Paul affirmed the devoted Christian workers with him and those in their midst (16:13-24).

The Lesson Passage

1. Giving Ourselves (15:58)

Verse 58 is an exhortation based on Paul's lengthy exposition on the resurrection of Jesus and believers. A proper understanding of the gospel, especially the implications of resurrection, should stimulate believers to become involved in ministry functions. Hope in resurrection should motivate believers to give their time, talents, and money to the Lord's work.

Verse 58: *Therefore, my beloved brethren, be steadfast, immovable, always abounding in the work of the Lord, knowing that your toil is not in vain in the Lord.*

A certain proverb says "Whenever you come across a 'therefore' in the Bible, look around and see what it is there for." In this verse the word **therefore** connects verse 58 to the chapter's statements on the resurrection. Paul had asserted that the resurrection of Jesus Christ had given Christians victory over sin and death. That conclusion should furnish Christians with the motivation to live their lives for Christ. Christ's loyalty to believers calls them to be loyal to Him as well.

Paul continued to address even the carnal Christians of Corinth as **beloved brethren.** Paul continued to love them even though the Corinthians had acted sinfully. Christians always should show each other courtesy and love. Even when they disagree or sin against one another, they still should love each other. Jesus taught that the exhibition of love to other believers authenticates a genuine relationship with Him (John 13:34-35).

A God who raises the dead deserves unqualified commitment from those who have trusted Christ. The command to **be steadfast** and **immovable** admonished the Corinthians to be stable in their thinking and actions. Their devotion to Christ should not be disturbed by the trends of society or by charismatic individuals. Such commitment spawns service and leads believers to be **always abounding in the work of the Lord**.

Serving the Lord is not always easy. Paul knew from experience that serving Christ often was tiring. He described ministry for the Lord as **toil.** The term denotes physical exhaustion induced by labor, exertion, or heat. Paul used the word 11 times. In fact, serving the Lord can be severe and exhausting labor. The word *vain* is the same Greek word used in 1 Corinthians 15:14. The word designates something that has no content and is ineffective.

The writer qualified believers' toil with the phrase *in the Lord.* Only God can generate success from Christian service. The efforts that were described here were done in the sphere of Christ. They were according to His revealed will and nature. Thus Paul encouraged the Corinthians with a reminder that even if the work was strenuous, it would not prove ineffective. It would prosper because Christ would secure the results.

2. Giving Our Resources (16:1-4)

The congregation in Corinth was not composed of the most affluent citizens in the city. Nonetheless, they were in a better financial state than the congregation in Jerusalem. The believers in that city were experiencing very difficult times.

Verse 1: *Now concerning the collection for the saints, as I directed the churches of Galatia, so do you also.*

In the first century, Christianity frequently attracted the lower levels of society. Its ideas of equality and freedom provided poor people and slaves with unexpected hope. And many were slaves who came to Christ; some were even destitute.

The gospel may offer only meager benefits in this world, but it promises a better life in the world to come. Pagan religions tended to be pessimistic about the afterlife. Within the Jewish community, the Sadducees denied the resurrection. And the Pharisees made the demands of righteousness an impossible dream. Into this void of despair, Christians preached their gospel of grace and love; and large numbers responded, especially the poor.

Jerusalem was the birthplace of Christianity. The city had an unusually large number of poor inhabitants. The impact of their acceptance of the good news about Jesus was profound. A large section of the city's population lived primarily or entirely on charity. For example, a majority of the scribes living in the city were dependent on subsidies. Vast numbers of other people renounced ordinary employment and devoted themselves to participation in religious ceremonies for profit. For a fee, these people would mourn at funerals or sing at weddings. Beggars proliferated around the temple. The city rightfully earned its reputation as a place of idlers.[1]

A significant segment of the working class in the city were day laborers. On average they earned about one denarius a day. During ordinary times their earnings were barely adequate. Failure to find work was catastrophic. During times of emergency caused by political instability or natural disaster, Jerusalem's already high cost of living rose steeply as profiteers exploited the situation.

A famine struck the region around A.D. 46 (Acts 11:28). The price of grain multiplied 16 times![2] Thus cost of the daily ration of grain was almost a day's wages. The number of those in poverty soared.

The burden of taxes also drained people's modest income. The Romans levied taxes to pay for government services and public works. The Jewish religious leaders required additional taxes to pay for the temple renovations then in progress.

In order to contend with the dire situation, believers helped one another. Christian charity was practiced. Christians with property or wealth sold assets and gave the money to the church for distribution to the poor (Acts 4:34-37). As these resources dwindled in the aftermath of the great famine, the need became greater and greater. To provide the funds that the Jerusalem congregation lacked, churches in other locations began to take up love offerings.

After Paul's first missionary journey, Christian representatives from various churches met in Jerusalem to discuss the conversion of Gentiles (Acts 15:1-35). The Jerusalem conference gave its stamp of approval to Paul's missionary efforts. The leaders of the Jewish congregation (James, Peter, and John) requested that Paul and Barnabas remember the poor. This was something Paul acknowledged that he already was eager to do (Gal. 2:10). From that occasion, he customarily took an offering in the churches he visited. The gifts were then delivered to Jerusalem. This offering was an excellent demonstration of Christian unity, a quality sadly lacking in Corinth.

Paul mentioned **Galatia** here to confirm that the practice was universal. He was on his third missionary journey when he wrote 1 Corinthians. Therefore, he had traveled through Galatia prior to coming to Ephesus (Acts 18:23).

Verse 2: *On the first day of every week each one of you is to put aside and save, as he may prosper, so that no collections be made when I come.*

Paul set forth some practical guidelines for Christian stewardship. First, giving should be systematic and regular. Paul admonished the Corinthians to give on **the first day of every week.** The instructions to **put aside and save** were administrative. The church could not disperse the funds until his arrival. Therefore, Paul instructed that the money was to be saved until needed. The money was not to be used for any purpose other than that for which it was designated. Paul also wanted to avoid a big fund-raising effort when he arrived in the city. Such activity might distract from the primary purpose of his visit, he thought. Financial concerns should always be kept secondary to spiritual goals.

Second, giving should be proportionate. The offering was to be determined by their income. Paul wrote that each member of the church at Corinth should give *as he may prosper.* This statement indicates that the Corinthians should make a contribution for the poor in Jerusalem in direct proportion to what they had earned.

Third, giving should be generous. Paul urged the believers to give liberally, even in their own poverty. However, they needed to remember that capability should determine the amount of their gift. God is more concerned with one's attitude than the amount of money given. He is not in need of our help to help Him provide for others. He already owns everything (Job 41:11; Ps. 50:12). *We* need to give.

Giving is an act of worship through which believers at Corinth expressed their dependence on God. The selection of *the first day of every week* is notable. Sunday is the day Christians celebrate the resurrection of Jesus. As we give, we confess our faith in God to provide for our needs. We, likewise, declare our appreciation to God for all He has done for us, especially for salvation (2 Cor. 9:15).

Verses 3-4: *When I arrive, whomever you may approve, I will send them with letters to carry your gift to Jerusalem; 4 and if it is fitting for me to go also, they will go with me.*

This instruction concerns a specific fund from the first century. However, there is a general principle here for every church. Church funds should be dispensed according to a church approved procedure of the highest ethical and moral accountability.

When I arrive communicated uncertainty about the exact time Paul would come to Corinth. Meanwhile, Paul wanted the church's financial policy to be thorough. The church was to honor its commitments without prior notification. This suggests that the commitment was not a concrete amount, but a proportional sum. It also required the records and deposits be current.

God's values are often not our values. We look at the bottom line and are awed by large figures. God looks at the attitude behind the gift (Mark 12:41-44). God repeatedly has demonstrated His ability to accomplish a great deal with a small quantity (Mark 8:1-9).

Whomever you may approve pointed out the church's responsibility to disbursing the money the church had collected. The money belonged to the church. Their commitment was to collect a *gift* for the saints in Jerusalem (16:1). Saints was a contemporary term for Christians. These church members in Jerusalem were complete strangers to the Corinthians. So the Corinthians were to insure that the entire gift reached the church in Jerusalem. Once turned over to that congregation, they were to trust its leaders to distribute the money to those individuals with the greatest need.

The Cooperative Program of the Southern Baptist Convention follows a similar outline. The local church selects people to collect and manage its weekly offerings. A percentage based on these receipts is then directed to the state convention. The local church members trust those individuals who serve God at the state and national level to ensure the funds are used for appropriate needs.

Paul promised that he would handle the offering by the highest ethical standards. He would travel with the offering and the designated Corinthians only *if it* was *fitting.*

3. Helping Others Serve (16:5-18)

Paul planned to visit Corinth in the near future. Although his travel plans were not complete, Paul desired that the Corinthian church share in his ministry.

Verse 5: *But I will come to you after I go through Macedonia, for I am going through Macedonia;*

Apparently, the Corinthians knew Paul intended to come to Corinth. They probably expected him to sail across the Aegean Sea and come directly to Corinth. Paul, however, informed them that his journey would include a trip through **Macedonia** first.

In this verse Paul reminded the Corinthians that he needed to minister to other churches as well as to their church. Because of the situation at Corinth when he first arrived, Paul decided not to accept financial support from the church he established. However, refusing their help bound him to live on what he could earn himself and what he received from other churches.

Verse 6: *and perhaps I will stay with you, or even spend the winter, so that you may send me on my way wherever I may go.*

Paul seems to have chosen to go to Macedonia first, not because of priority in need, but so that he would be free to spend more time in Corinth. The church at Philippi was the primary church in Macedonia, and it was a congregation with which Paul enjoyed a healthy relationship. He suggested he might **spend the winter** in Corinth. Severe winter storms and difficult navigation prevented travel at sea. The climate also discouraged travel by land.

One result Paul hoped to gain from his visit to Corinth was support for his next missionary endeavor. He disclosed this goal when he wrote **that you may send me on my way wherever I may go.** Similar expressions occur in Acts 15:3; Romans 15:24; and 3 John 6. They all involve travel and ministry and imply financial and spiritual support for his missionary ventures. Thus Paul was requesting that the Corinthian believers support his work in missions. He had not determined yet in what geographical location that work might be. But even uncertainty about God's direction for his ministry was to be no hindrance to their financial support (or their prayer support) during this period of uncertainty about future plans.

Verse 7: *For I do not wish to see you now just in passing; for I hope to remain with you for some time, if the Lord permits.*

Paul expressed his hope to remain in Corinth for an extended period. The time of year he arrived, however, would be a factor in the length of his stay there. We already have noted the cessation of travel during the winter. Therefore, travel schedules to Paul's winter destination (wherever it might have been) would determine the time available at stops along the way.

Paul qualified his desire to make his stay at Corinth a lengthy one by *if the Lord permits.* The apostle recognized God's sovereignty over his life. A multitude of circumstances might modify his plans, and Paul understood those changes to be under God's control. Christians, too, always should recognize that they do not control their lives. Therefore, all plans should be contingent on God's will. And whenever God's sovereignty prevents the fulfillment of plans, every Christian should see the Lord's hand in the events.

Verse 8: *But I will remain in Ephesus until Pentecost;*

Pentecost was the second of the three annual feasts prescribed in the law of Moses. In the Old Testament Era it was known as the Feast of Weeks (Ex. 34:22), the Feast of Harvest (Ex. 23:16), and the day of the first fruits (Num. 28:26). It occurred seven weeks, or 50 days, after Passover. Hence, it acquired the popular name of Pentecost.

Pentecost was celebrated in early June. If Paul remained in Asia Minor until after Pentecost and he stopped at Philippi, Thessalonica, and Berea, he would arrive in Corinth in late summer or early fall.

Verse 9: *for a wide door for effective service has opened to me, and there are many adversaries.*

Paul wished to remain in Ephesus until Pentecost because of an opportunity for successful ministry there. The verb *has opened* implies that the door was opened at some point in the past and remained open in the present. The adjective *effective* means "active." By this word Paul referred to the operation of God in his life and ministry. Here, the adjective refers to the divinely directed possibilities of missionary work.[3] Paul's preaching and witnessing since his arrival in Ephesus were producing spiritual results in the lives of the Ephesians. The power of God was being manifested clearly in his efforts. Therefore, Paul was encouraged; and he desired to continue ministering there as long as feasible. It would not have been God's will, Paul thought, to walk away prematurely from the obvious blessing of God on his efforts at that time.

In addition to his success in preaching the gospel of Christ, Paul had encountered *many adversaries.* Opposition to him was growing. Eventually, the opposition would swell into the great riot described in Acts 19:23-41). As they opposed Paul, the mob shouted, "Great is Artemis of the Ephesians!" The danger to Paul's life was real, and he wanted the church at Corinth to pray for his success and personal safety.

In 1 Corinthians 16:10-19 Paul commented on several individuals familiar to the Corinthians. He had dispatched Timothy to Corinth to assist in resolving the plight of the church there (see Introduction). Paul was concerned that the Corinthians might mistreat Timothy, his younger associate. Therefore, the apostle requested that the Corinthians to treat Timothy as they would him (16:10-11). Paul also informed the church that its former minister, Apollos, did not wish to return to Corinth in the immediate future (16:12).

After an admonition to behave like loving adults, Paul commented about certain members of the Corinthian church. He advised the congregation to listen to the counsel of those Christians whose experience and ministry revealed genuine spiritual maturity (16:15-16). Paul also acknowledged that the recent visit by some of these individuals had been of personal benefit to himself (16:17-18).

4. Conclusion (16:19-24)

Paul noted that the churches in the region around Ephesus sent their respects to their sister church at Corinth. Christians should be interested and concerned about the work of Christ, wherever it might be. Naturally, he mentioned Aquila and Priscilla because they had helped establish the Corinthian church.

The kiss was an ancient gesture of friendship, acceptance, and respect. This customary greeting was widely used among Christians as an expression of love and the unity of fellowship. In our modern western world, it has its equivalent in the handshake.

Paul wrote verses 21 through 24 himself. The preceding portion of the letter was dictated to a secretary. This scribe wrote Paul's words on paper. Having completed his dictation, Paul picked up the pen, signed his name, and wrote a few brief remarks. His signature authenticated the letter (2 Thess. 3:17).

Paul's first comment was a curse on anyone who did not love the Lord. He was deeply distressed to think that some of his readers truly did not love Jesus Christ. Paul followed this comment with the term **Maranatha.** This word is a transliteration of an Aramaic expression. Translated, it means, "Our Lord, come!" It is a prayer for the second coming of Jesus.

Paul's final words were a benediction in which he invoked the grace of the Lord Jesus and expressed his own love for the Corinthians in Christ Jesus. Jesus is the Lord; He is divine. He also is human. Through Him God had extended His unmerited favor to the Corinthians. Through Him God had expressed His unqualified love to the Corinthians. Through Jesus, God's grace and love are ours too.

For Further Study

1. Read about Paul's ministry in Ephesus as it was recorded by Luke in Acts 18:23-19:41. Who are some missionaries for whom you can pray for their success and safety?

2. Read about ships, sailors, and navigation in the *Holman Bible Dictionary,* pages 1269-1273, or in another Bible dictionary.

3. Read "Rich and Poor in the First Century," in the Fall 1990 issue of the *Biblical Illustrator.*

4. Read "The Persecutions Paul Suffered," in the Summer 1992 issue of the *Biblical Illustrator.*

---

1 Joachim Jeremias, *Jerusalem in the Time of Jesus:* An Investigation into Economic and Social Conditions during the New Testament Period, trans. F. H. and C. H. Cave (Philadelphia, Pennsylvania: Fortress Press, 1969), 111-19.

2 Jeremias, *Jerusalem in the Time of Jesus,* 123.

3 *Theological Dictionary of the New Testament,* 1964 ed., "εργόν" by Gerhard Delling, 2:653.